Remarkable Women of Devon

First published in Great Britain by The Mint Press, 2009

ISBN 978-1-903356-59-3

Cataloguing in Publication Data

CIP record for this title is available from the British Library

The Mint Press
Taddyforde House South
Taddyforde Estate
New North Road
Exeter, Devon
England EX4 4AT
Email: sales@themintpress.co.uk
www.stevensbooks.co.uk

Typeset by Kestrel Data
Cover design by Delphine Jones

Printed and bound in Great Britain
by Short Run Press Ltd, Exeter

Remarkable Women of Devon

TODD GRAY

TODD GRAY

Contents

Acknowledgements	vii
Foreword	xi
Introduction	1
Rachel, Countess of Bath, of Tawstock	9
The Amazonian Sirens of Shaldon and Teignmouth	13
Lady Lucy Reynell of Forde House, Newton Abbot	20
The Seven Women of Mol's Coffee House	23
Wilmot and Thomasin Moreman of Exmoor, two Georgian scolds by Andrew Brice of Exeter	25
Miss Anne Hamilton of late Georgian Exeter, a 'gentlewoman of the old school'	38
Maria Foote of Plymouth, and Countess of Harrington	40
Mary Anne Burges of Awliscombe	44
Granny Scott and Betsy Gammon of Ilfracombe	49
Hannah Cowley, Tiverton's Playwright	53
The Misses Parminters	54
Joanna Southcott, Gittisham's Prophet	56
Sarah Catherine Martin and Old Mother Hubbard of Kitley	59
Anne Perriam, Exmouth's 'Warrior Woman'	65
Elizabeth Ann Holman, a Devon navvy	67

Mrs Partington of Sidmouth 72

Louisa, Lady Rolle, of Bicton 77

Amelia Griffiths, Queen of Algologists 80

Viscountess Beaconsfield: from Mary Evans of Brampford Speke
to Mrs Benjamin Disraeli of 10 Downing Street 82

Benjamin Disraeli's other Devon woman: Mrs Sarah Brydges
Willyams of Torquay 86

Two female pharmacists in Victorian Paignton 90

The Misses Skinners and their Hotel of Rest for Women in
Business at Babbacombe, 1878 to 1971 91

Two Devonport Dames: Aggie Weston and Sophie Wintz, the
Sailors' Friends 99

Women's emancipation and the struggle for rights 107

The Election at Newton Abbot, 1907 to 1908 110

The Prime Minister at Clovelly Court in 1909 113

The arrest of three Suffragettes at Exeter in 1909 115

The Pilgrimage to London in 1913 117

Mrs Pankhurst's Hunger Strike at Exeter Prison in 1913 120

Dr Mabel Ramsay, Medical Doctor, Suffragette and Soroptomist 123

Elsie May Fraser, A Devonport V. A. D. nurse 127

Exeter's first female strikers 131

Lady Nancy Astor 132

Dorothy Elmhirst of Dartington Hall 135

Agatha Christie 139

My Lady of the Moor: Olive Katherine Parr as Beatrice Chase 140

Who was Who in Devonshire in 1934 142

Women at work on the Home Front in the Second World War 145

Conclusion 151

Notes 153

Index 162

Acknowledgements

This book has been in the making for more than fifteen years. In that time I have been collecting material on a wide number and variety of women and from a great many places. Not all of it has been appropriate to this book but I hope all of those who feature in this collection will be seen to be remarkable in some way. Over the years I have had the great help of a considerable number of people in archives and libraries. I would like to take this opportunity to thank the staffs of the three record offices in Devon, particularly Tim Wormleighton who has once again been very patient, and also those at Maidstone, Taunton and Bristol. Lately I have received valuable help from Kevin Bolton of Manchester City Archives, Peter Basham of the Archive of the Royal College of Physicians and Julie Wakefield of the Museum of the Royal Pharmaceutical Society. To all of them I am grateful. Devon's library staff has also answered many questions over the years and I owe a debt to those of the North Devon Athenaeum, Westcountry Studies Library, the Torbay Reference Library, Exeter Central Library and the Plymouth Local Studies Library. I would also like to thank Naomi Ayre, Peter Christie, John Draisey, Terry Leaman, Margaret Reed, Margery Rowe and Dr Lawrence Normand for their personal help and advice. Finally, I am grateful to the members of Tuesday morning class for their patience and helpful comments.

Illustration Sources

Foreword

I am delighted that Devon County Council has been able to support this new book which highlights the all too often overlooked part that women have played in shaping the history of Devon. There have of course been numerous of books published over the centuries on people in Devon's history. John Prince's *Worthies of Devon* (1701) and Sabine Baring Gould's *Devonshire Characters and Strange Events* (1908) are just two that come to mind. But these books have tended largely to focus on the male contribution to our history. This new book helps to redress the balance!

In writing this book, Dr Gray draws on years of specialist research into the archives of Devon. He has again demonstrated his skill in opening new areas of study – the 'hidden history' of Devon – for people to discover and to learn from. His previous publications such as *Devon & The Slave Trade* have quite rightly been recognised by winning awards.

This book also draws attention to the richness of the archives and reference collections that Devon possesses. In my role as the County Council's Executive Member for Culture, I am continually impressed by the breadth of the collections held in the Devon Record Office, the Westcountry Studies Library and other Devon archives and libraries – and by the expertise and commitment of the staff who look after them.

I was especially pleased that the Devon Record Office was last year able to acquire – for the benefit of the nation and with a major grant from the National Heritage Memorial Fund – the Sidmouth

Papers, the nationally significant archive of the 19th century Prime Minister, Henry Addington. I would encourage anyone reading this book to visit the Devon Record Office in Exeter to explore this archive, which contains among other documents an outstanding series of letters from Admiral Lord Nelson.

The County Council is grant-aiding this book as part of its commitment to celebrating Devon's culture. I hope that readers, both male and female, will find the stories Todd Gray charts in its pages full of inspiration and interest. One thing they all have in common is that they show us how individuals – not just organisations – can do so much to help make a difference to the society in which we all live.

Councillor Sheila Hobden
Executive Member for Culture
Devon County Council
February 2009

Introduction

It would probably be difficult for most Devonians to list a dozen remarkable women from the county's past. This is a much easier for notable men: histories of Devon are full of noteworthy men with many, such as Sir Francis Drake, Sir Walter Raleigh, Joshua Reynolds, Nicholas Hilliard and Charles Kingsley, having made a marked personal contribution far beyond the county. But women are less frequently featured and it is less easy to compose an equivalent list of notable women.

It could be argued that Devon has had, over the centuries, few women who can be shown to have been remarkable. This has nothing to do with their actual abilities or achievements but merely with the fact that until recently few women were recorded in original records: no doubt there were remarkable women but substantiating it is very difficult. Women were also denied the public role which helps makes them visible to historians: until modern times men held public offices and were not as restricted in the independent careers which have helped to distinguish them. Most memoirs and autobiographies have also been written by men.

What qualifies all of the several dozen women therefore who feature in this book is that historical evidence has survived which shows something significant can be discovered of their lives. Some can be described as remarkable in that they had notable life histories: for example the fishing women of Teignmouth led largely independent and very unusual existences which they themselves created. Likewise, Elizabeth Holman chose to don male attire presumably in order to achieve her independence by gaining a higher wage. Her way of life was obviously difficult but it was one to which she was very dedicated. Ann Perriam from Exmouth also lived very much within a male environment. There was also Mary Evans, Exeter-born and from a moderate background, but who rose to become the wife of a Prime Minister and was created a Countess. Maria Foote also rose to the aristocracy after humble beginnings in Plymouth. Other Devon women, such as Lady Nancy Astor at Plymouth and Mrs Dorothy Elmhirst at Dartington, had great wealth which provided them with the means to achieve. They rank as some of the most high profile Devonians of the twentieth century and yet both were born in America. Each woman made extraordinary contributions to Devon although they were on opposite sides of the political spectrum. Agatha Christie is probably one of the most well-known Devon women to have achieved outstanding success, can certainly be termed remarkable and who also had American ancestry. Thus, the three most famous Devon women of early twentieth century Devon, Astor, Elmhirst and Christie, had foreign backgrounds.

Other women in this collection are far less familiar and some will be completely unknown to modern society. They are no less deserving to have their place in history recorded. The Misses Skinners of Babbacombe, for example, should have been lauded many years ago. Their House of Rest For Women In Business was an extraordinary achievement and became their life work. Some of the women in this collection have stories which are inspirational, such as the Georgian owners of Mol's Coffee House or the Victorian Dames Agatha Weston and Sophia Wintz, and all should be regarded as part of a neglected field of Devon's history.

It is unfortunate that very little of any consequence can be said of the individual lives of most of the millions of women who have lived in Devon over the last five hundred years but the survival of information about some of them allows us to learn something of their particular experiences. Those in this collection cannot be said to be representative in any way and it is not intended that by naming these women as remarkable that many others did not also have notable lives but in this vast area of historical darkness there are these few pinpricks, as dim as some of them are, which shed light on random individuals and the historical moment of which they were a part.

Only women who are no longer alive have been considered for inclusion in this book. Widening it to those alive today would have transformed it from a historical study to a 'Who is Who in Devon'. They have also been dead for some time: the book relies more on the historical past rather than the immediate last few decades. In a few years the contribution of some women who have recently died will become clearer; with time the legacy of Beryl Cook and Mary Wesley for example will become easier to understand.

One of the difficulties in compiling a list of women with remarkable lives in Devon is the longstanding neglect of women's history in the county. It began with the county's first historian. In the late 1500s, when John Hooker described the people of Devon, he noted the population in male terms: he commented upon the various social classes but only mentioned men. His work was hugely influential and subsequent writers parroted his view of society. One seventeenth-century writer noted the county's inhabitants comprised gentlemen, merchants, yeoman, artificers, mechanics and labourers. There were no women.[1] Likewise, the Reverend John Prince a hundred years later, managed to write his *Worthies of Devon* without including a single woman.[2] In 1716 he had the opportunity to rectify this in his second volume but again only men were considered to be Worthies. Prince's prime intention was 'to record those persons (be they of ancient families or none at all) who were eminent in their generations for arts or arms, for learning or for prowess or some other extraordinary accomplishment.'[3] His work has become a key text on Devon's history and remains hugely influential but it is telling that Prince could write his book without any apparent comment, then or since, on the lack of any women.[4] It may not have occurred to him to include women, he might not have known of any likely candidates or it is possible, but improbable, that he deliberately omitted them.

Women have largely remained invisible to Devon's historians:

Prince's failure to notice women has been commonplace. Perhaps the earliest commentator to address this was the editor of one of Devon's seventeenth-century historians who in 1785 criticised him for neglecting women. He wrote 'it may be deemed an unpardonable omission' to only write of men and noted he thought that no county 'produces more agreeable women and that they are nowhere excelled in beauty, wit, industry or any other amiable qualities'.[5]

It is interesting that the Victorian Women's Window in Exeter Cathedral is not of local women but of 'seven women of holy scripture'.[6] Devon's most famous female saint, Sidwella, might have been appropriate but was not considered in the early 1880s for the window. Ordinary women were obviously not deemed to be inspirational and in any case the cathedral was already littered with monuments to wealthy men and women. Perhaps it was considered too difficult or controversial to find women, even amongst the leading families of Devon, who made publicly-lauded contributions.

There is still very little on women's experiences in Devon in spite of many women now writing local history. One of the earliest to consider women was Dr Ruth Easterling who compiled, sometime in the 1930s, a card index of references to medieval women in Devon. Nearly all historians of Devon write of general society without considering what might have been a separate female contribution or issue; few have looked specifically at distinct experiences of women.[7] Little or no consideration, for example, has been paid to the activities of the county's Suffragettes.[8]

The intention of this work is to address this neglect by introducing short studies of various women who have made remarkable personal contributions to Devon. These vignettes do not form, in any way, a history of women in Devon but may introduce individuals to readers hitherto unfamiliar with them and indicate a contribution which has been overlooked. It has been written from the perspective of an historian of Devon with the hope that it might encourage further research on other women.

The lack of women's history is surprising when one considers women have outnumbered men in Devon as elsewhere for at least the last two hundred years. Census records show females have comprised from 52 to 54 per cent of the population.

Numbers of females and males in Devon, 1801 to 1991[9]

	Females	Males	Total	Percentage female
1801	185,761	157,240	343,001	54.2
1811	203,755	179,553	383,308	53.2
1821	230,811	208,229	439,040	52.6
1831	258,689	235,789	494,478	52.3
1841	280,979	252,752	533,731	52.6
1851	297,515	269,583	567,098	52.5
1861	304,962	279,411	584,373	52.2
1871	316,126	285,248	601,374	52.6
1881	318,255	285,340	603,595	52.7
1891	333,910	297,898	631,808	52.8
1901	349,680	312,536	662,216	52.8
1911	366,890	332,813	699,703	52.4
1921	377,462	332,026	709,488	53.2
1931	387,081	345,887	732,968	52.8
1941	census not taken			
1951	419,462	378,276	797,738	52.6
1961	433,138	389,561	822,699	52.7
1971	471,621	426,783	898,404	52.5
1981	496,600	455,400	952,000	52.2
1991	529,469	486,500	1,015,969	52.1

In the middle of the nineteenth century the discrepancy in numbers was commented upon throughout the country and one (male) Victorian writer even suggested the imbalance should be corrected by sending women abroad; emigration was seen as the key to this 'excess' population.[10] It was at this time that many Devonians, including of course women, were already emigrating to the United States or to British colonies. It has not been determined whether any women emigrated because they were considered 'excess' population.

One way in which women have left their own records behind them is through their cook books. There are a number of these manuscripts which contain recipes. One example is that written by Deborah Symes from 1764. She noted in her commonplace book a recipe for mincemeat.

> 'take one pound of suet, one pound of currants washed and dried, half pound of best raisins, half a nutmeg, one penny worth mace, half dozen golden pippins, half a lemon, pint Madeira wine'.[11]

There are many other such examples, evidence of the domestic chores and responsibilities which occupied the lives of most women. Fortunately these records of the domestic world reveal insights into what would otherwise be considered unremarkable lives.

Some women can be found in records which show them as victims of injustice. Perhaps the most striking example is the persecution of three North Devon women for witchcraft. In 1792, a little more than a hundred years after it happened, one Devon writer noted 'in the year 1682 three poor friendless old women of this town named Temperance Lloyd, Mary Trembles and Susannah Edwards were accused by their cruel, ignorant neighbours of being witches.' He concluded these 'unhappy creatures fell victims to ignorance, prejudice and superstition being all three executed at Exeter the same year'.[12] It could be argued that their lives were not remarkable but their deaths were in themselves and were the last vestiges of social prejudice that came at the end of centuries of witchcraft persecution.

Random records survive which provide a bare framework into a woman's life but little else. For example, in Ashburton's Anglican churchyard is the memorial stone for Miriam Adams, a post-woman who travelled her rounds on her donkey Betsy.

'This tablet is erected to the memory of Miriam Adams who for forty-four years discharged her responsible duties of letter carrier to the post office in this town with uniform cheerfulness and strict fidelity. She died October 12th, 1858, aged 77.'[13]

A trace of the voices of some women can occasionally be heard. For instance, when in 1892 at a religious meeting for women only at Bishopsteignton one of those present said 'Us wants something of this sort, it does us good, brightens us up, and makes us feel we are somebody and can do something.'[14] Positive and inspirational words can be found from the past, notably from the Suffragettes in the very early 1900s, but much can also be discovered of the discrimination faced by women. For example, there was nothing unusual in 1922 about the decision of the Torquay Education Committee that female teachers who married would have their service terminated.[15] They, and many others, were greatly restricted in their choices. Some, as will be seen in the pages that followed, faced similar struggles while others were wealthy enough to overcome many of the difficulties that their gender normally brought. However, all of these women led lives that were individual and noteworthy and left their mark in the historical records all for very distinct reasons.

For Kate

Rachel, Countess of Bath, of Tawstock

Of the many thousands of women who lived in seventeenth-century Devon the most is known about Rachel, Countess of Bath. For some forty years she lived in North Devon at Tawstock, the ancestral home of the family of her husband, Henry, the fifth Earl of Bath. Both were strangers to Devon: he was born in Ireland, and came to the title unexpectedly, while she was born in Kent and raised at Apethorpe in Northamptonshire. Even so, as the owners of the most extensive estate in Devon they had positions of power which made them of great interest not only in North Devon but throughout the region. It could be argued that Lady Rachel was the stronger personality of the two and she successfully overcame the events which engulfed them shortly after their marriage.

Lady Rachel was born in 1613, the daughter of Sir Anthony Fane. Her husband Henry Bourchier was twice her age at their marriage: she was 25 and he was 51 years old. Eight months later, in July 1639, she came to Devon. Her arrival was keenly awaited: shortly beforehand her husband wrote 'your presence is much desired in Devonshire and many services presented by those that never saw you'. Lady Rachel was then Devon's only resident Countess and Tawstock remained her main home until she died in 1680.

It is only through a quirk of fate that so much is known of Lady Rachel. Her husband died in May 1655 and less than nine months later she remarried. This time she was the older bride, at 42, while her husband, Lionel Cranfield, third Earl of Middlesex, was only thirty years old. It is because of this second marriage, or more to

Rachel, Countess of Bath

the point, because of the subsequent unhappiness of the pair, that the details of Rachel's life are known. Six years after the marriage Lady Rachel was granted a separation on grounds of desertion and cruelty. Her young husband was the subject of gossip in that he was accused of leading an immoral life. Lord Middlesex was, however, directly responsible for ensuring she has a unique place in Devon's history. During the breakdown of their marriage the earl refused his wife's request to return her own personal, family and estate papers. Because of this her large collection of documents remained in Kent and, most importantly, was not at Tawstock when the house was later completely destroyed by fire. They remain in Kent today, more than three hundred years after the couple's marital disagreement. Therefore, by chance rather than by design, more is known of Lady Rachel than of any other member of her first husband's family.

Lady Rachel may not have been lucky in love. Her first marriage only lasted sixteen years. Affectionate love letters survive from him, in which he called her 'dear heart', 'dear girl', 'sweet girl' and 'sweet heart', but within a few years of their marriage the country descended into the Civil War and his prominence as a Royalist caused her considerable difficulties through the 1640s and 1650s. The fifth Earl of Bath became a member of the Privy Council in 1641 and later held the Privy Seal. Just before war was declared in 1642 he tried to mobilise support for the King in Devon and travelled to Exeter where he was coolly received. Although the owner of the largest local estate the earl was still an outsider and moreover not known for his skills with people: Clarendon later described his 'sour-tempered unsocial behaviour'. He was not able to influence Devonians to support the Royalist cause. Two months after returning home from Exeter the earl was arrested in North Devon and sent to London where he was imprisoned in the Tower of London. It was at this point that Lady Rachel appears to have run her husband's large estate and their homes in Devon and London. The earl was dependent upon his wife during his ten months in the Tower and she continued to support him even during their later flight from a Parliamentary army into the far west of Cornwall.

Tawstock was Devon's grandest house at this time with a great medieval deer park on one side and an ornamental garden on the other. Among her accounts are several lists of the many rooms with their contents which show rich furnishings including several dozen tapestries, an ebony mirror, globes, a 'mathematical jewel', Persian and Turkish carpets, Spanish furniture, musical instruments (two violes, an Irish harp and a violin) and a large number of landscape paintings. Her own portrait was painted a number of times including by Cornelius Johnson and Sir Anthony van Dyck. Several have survived.

Her papers reveal her interests: she loved games of all sorts. Outdoors she played bowls and troll madam while inside she played chess, dice, loadum, a form of backgammon and almost continually at cards.[16] She is now known for the writing of a masque which was performed in about 1625, during the Christmas season, for the household.[17] Her papers also show a great interest in religion and in reading including poetry.

It was expected that a woman in her position was interested in giving charity but Lady Rachel appears to have been particularly devoted to it. The inscription on her memorial proclaims her interest in children. Lady Rachel:

> 'although she was childless yet she was parent to more than a thousand children, whom in a very genteel manner she brought up, gave them portions, consecrated and even ennobled. She still lives, and never will die, while any spark of gratitude remains in this country.'

Her personal accounts provide evidence of her largess. There are quarterly payments to two individuals for teaching children to read and write. She sent Jonathan Pickard to school in nearby Barnstaple, probably at the Grammar School. She had taken him in as an orphaned infant. Her records show a further ten children were brought into the household: three were aged eight, one was not yet six and another less than five years old. She also maintained a French boy and had a ward as well. Her care of Ned Lewin is particularly interesting: he came from Northampton and she called him 'my boy'. He was a baby of three months when she began caring for him. Eventually she had him apprenticed to a local shoemaker.

Lady Rachel died in London in 1680 and her body was returned to Tawstock where she was buried. Her memorial statue was a gift from the diocese of Bath and Wells. The countess retained a devotion to Devon long after her husband, who brought her there, had died. Her memorial noted 'in domestic, civil and religious affairs she had a genius exceeding that of a man'. [18]

The Amazonian Sirens of Shaldon and Teignmouth

One part of Devon has distinguished itself, not just from the rest of the county but also from the rest of Britain, in its women participating in maritime work. Female activity in fishing, in particular, can be traced back more than four hundred years: in 1600 the people from Torquay and Stokeinteignhead who were collecting oysters at Shaldon were almost all women.[19] 'Oyster women' were a traditional sight along Devon's estuaries but one eighteenth-century visitor was surprised by them 'with feet and legs entirely naked, straw bonnets of uncouth shapes tied on their heads . . . strolling along with wide mannish strides to the borders of the river'.[20] The women fishing at the mouth of the Teign were very different.

By the 1500s Devon had an extensive network of fisheries. Most were overseas, including off Ireland, Iceland, Newfoundland and New England, but there were a number of fisheries onshore. Men supplied the labour for nearly all of it. Women, when they occasionally joined the men in pulling the fishing net onto the shore received a share in the overall profit.[21] However, along the river Teign the women were not helping the men but doing the entire work themselves. The Reverend John Skinner was just one of many commentators fascinated by these female fishers. He wrote in 1797:

'After breakfast we saw thirteen salmon caught on one drought. It is peculiar to this place, I believe, that the women alone are employed in salmon fishery, there being eight nets

Women at the mouth of the Teign, by T. H. Williams, 1820s

in the village, and eight women to each net. Every fourth fish that is caught is the right of the Lord of the Manor, and every person who chooses to fish, complying with this custom, has permission to make use of as many nets as he thinks fit, which rather surprised me when I saw none but females. But the men, I believe are chiefly employed in piloting ships or in other fisheries.'[22]

The reason for these women fishing in the Teign lay in the port's heavy involvement in Canadian fishing. In 1773 Maria Burney wrote to her sister Fanny, famous for her novels, that:

'you see nothing here but women in the summer, their husbands all go out to the Newfoundland fishery, for eight or nine months in the year so the women do all the laborious business, such as rowing and towing the boats, and go out a fishing yet I never saw more cleaner cottages nor healthier fine children. The women are in general handsome, none

14

plain though tall and strapping owing to their robust work. The husbands come home about November or December, consequently winter is the time for their mirth and jollity. They are very poor yet no signs of poverty appear nor have I seen a beggar since I came'.[23]

The most famous commentator was Fanny Burney. She wrote in 1773 that a friend had commented that he:

'could not have imagined such a race of females existed in a civilized country and had he come hither by sea, he should have almost fancied he had been cast on a new discovered coast. They caught this evening at one time 9 large salmon, a John Dory and a gurnard. On Tuesday evening we went again and saw them catch 4 dozen mackerel at a haul'.[24]

She was obviously taken with the women. Burney also noted:

'We all went on Monday evening to the seashore to see the seine drawn: this is a most curious work and all done by women. They have a very long net, so considerable as to cost them 13 or 16 pounds – this they first draw into a boat, which they go off the shore in and row in a kind of semi-circle, till they land at some distance; all the way, they spread this net, one side of which is kept above water by corks. Then they land, and divide forces. Half of them return to the beginning of the net and half remain at the end and then with amazing strength, they, both divisions, at the same time, pull the net in by the two ends. Whatever fish they catch are always encircled in the middle of the net which comes out of the water the last and as they draw towards each other they all join in getting their prey. When once they perceive that there is fish in their nets, they set up a loud shout and make an almost unintelligible noise in quarrelling, their joy in disputing at the same time upon their shares and on what fish escaped them'.[25]

15

Fanny Burney, an observer of the Teign women

Teignmouth was then being transformed from a fishing port to a resort and the town was full of these genteel visitors dumbfounded by this spectacle of women fishing.

Women were also employed in ferrying passengers across the Teign between Shaldon and Teignmouth. In the summer of 1816 the improbably named Augustus Toplady wrote 'I witnessed the novel sight of Amazonian Seamen, we were not only ferried across by a woman but the sight soon became familiar, for the numerous boats I observed similarly navigated and managed with the most surprising skill and adroitness.'[26] There were also similar women nearby at Coombe Cellars, a few miles up the estuary towards Newton Abbot. Reverend John Swete commented on the ferry in 1795. It:

Swete's Herculean comparison
with the Teign women

'has been managed for half a century by a weather-beaten female and her daughters whose constitutions are proof to the roughest storms and whose iron aspect seems to belie their claims to that sex, whose appellation is *soft and fair*. With such frame of body and kindred mind they are fit tenants in the boisterous months of winter for these exposed habitations.'[27]

Fortunately these visitors to the resort were sufficiently intrigued to describe the women at length. In 1782 John Mount wrote 'the river Teign divides Teignmouth from a country village called Shaldon, over which are ferry boats continually passing, all rowed by women whose dress alone distinguishes them from the other sex, for their complexions and figures are equally coarse and athletic'.[28] Ten years later Reverend Swete commented:

'The boat soon arrived manned by two women whose muscular system, as far as I could see, appeared to have been moulded after the Hercules Farnese. The female inhabitants of this salutary and piscine shore from being accustomed to draw their subsistence in nets from the bosom of the ocean, have acquired all that firmness of tone in their bodies and that intrepidity of mind peculiar to the Sons of Neptune – shooting their seines, rowing and navigating their boats with as much dexterity and spirit as any British Tar'.[29]

Reverend Skinner also noted 'these women are dressed in large trousers like the Dutch and when they are drawing the seine, they pull off their shoes and stockings and altogether are no very captivating sirens'.[30] Fanny Burney wrote the fullest description:

'They are all robust and well made, and have remarkably beautiful teeth and some of them are really very fine women; their dress is barbarous; they have stays half-laced and something by way of handkerchiefs about their necks, they wear a coloured flannel or stuff petticoat; no shoes or stockings notwithstanding the hard pebbles and stones all along the beach and their coat is pinned up in the shape of a pair of trousers, leaving them wholly naked to the knee.'[31]

Irrespective of the financial or social imperatives that drew them to fishing, some of the women at least seemed to thrive on it. Reverend John Skinner spoke to the women and related, in 1797, of one of their lives:

'They told me an anecdote of one, rather a fine girl, who was put out to service in a very good place, but never happy till she returned to her old associates and she is now engaged with the rest in this laborious manner of gaining her livelihood.'[32]

By 1773 the women of Shaldon and Teignmouth were rowing against one another in the local regatta: Fanny Burney wrote 'the Teignmouth games concluded the day after with a rowing match between the women of Shaldon, a fishing town on the other side of the Teign, and the fair ones of this place'.[33] It may have been in memory of these early women that in the late 1800s female rowers named themselves the Teignmouth Amazons.[34]

Lucy Reynell of Forde, Newton Abbot

Lady Lucy Reynell may have been typical of many other gentry women in Devon in the seventeenth century but what distinguishes her from them is that she has left behind her account book. It provides unusual insights into her life and of those who lived in her household. It also shows women selling fish from Teignmouth, possibly from one of the local 'Amazons'.

Lucy Brandon was born in about 1578 in London. Her father was a wealthy merchant and in about 1600 she married Richard Reynell, a Devon lawyer who had been successful in London. He was some twenty years older and was knighted in 1622. Three years later they hosted King Charles I as he travelled to Plymouth in what was the first royal visit to Devon in more than a hundred years. Their home was conveniently located near the main road south of Dartmoor from Exeter to Plymouth and the house had recently been renovated. The plaster ceilings, which survive today, must have impressed even the Stuart courtiers.

For the royal party that September of 1625 the Reynells prepared two bucks, three John Dories, 2 mullets, 2 gurnards, 25 peel, 2 salmon, 17 soles, 140 partridges, 7 pheasants, 61 chickens, 46 capons, 10 ducks, 4 pullets, 6 geese, 71 turkeys, 28 pigeons, 1 pea-hen, 2 mallards, 10 plovers, 1 gull, 36 larks, 38 rabbits and a hare. On the return visit from Plymouth the King's company were given six oxen and kine as well as five sheep.

Lady Reynell's account book shows that the household ate well irrespective of royal visitors. Of particular importance was the

Lady Lucy Reynell of
Forde House, c.1600

saltwater fish from the nearby Teign estuary. Great amounts were
consumed including a mussel only found in England in that river.
The book shows frequent travel to Exeter, where the couple had a
townhouse, and to London where she must have visited her friends
and family.

Sir Richard died in 1634 and Lady Lucy was left to run the
household. During the Civil War she hosted both Royalists and
Roundheads and at one point Oliver Cromwell stayed. She never
remarried and her monument is one she shares with her husband.
Her account book shows a payment to the mason 'if he performs
it well to my liking, else ten pounds is to be deducted'. An early
portrait shows her in her prime: she was a thin, beautiful, dark-
haired woman. Lady Lucy did not die until 1652, nearly twenty years
after her husband. In 1634 she had their monument constructed as

a bed with the two of them beside one another. The mason sculpted her husband and apparently left a gap for her own stone figure to be sculpted when she died. It appears as though he estimated the space on the stone bed as she was in 1634, at age 56, but it is likely that on her death, aged 74, she had put on substantial weight. This would account for her husband now being pushed out to the edge of their death bed and hanging over the side with not enough room to rest comfortably.

Shortly after Lady Lucy's death her nephew wrote *The Life and Death of the Religious and Virtuous Lady, the Lady Lucie Reynell, of Ford in Devon, who died the 18th of April 1652.* In it he stresses how pious she was, notes her charity to the poor and her hard work. One long passage concerns her sewing particularly for the needy. The description of her could easily illustrate the ideal gentry woman. A later commentator, after having visited the house, noted the opulence of the rooms and commented on how the family name died out that generation. He likened the Reynells to a meteor blazing with a brilliance that was of but 'short duration'. [35] In the house she reconstructed, in the monument she had built for her husband and in the household account book the life of Lady Lucy Reynell can be rediscovered.

Lady Lucy's memorial image

The seven women of Mol's Coffee House

Only a few doors away from Lady Reynell's townhouse in Exeter stood a building which, several generations later, would house a business which lasted more than a hundred years and was successful only through the ingenuity of women.

For much of the last century, and part of the one before, a tall tale about Mol's Coffee House has obscured the facts about this business which ran through nearly the entirety of the Georgian period. In the early 1700s a coffee house was established in this medieval building in Cathedral Close in Exeter and continued to operate until 1837. It became popular with gentry and merchants of the city and county. They subscribed to the business and were allowed access to what were the first newspapers from the coaches arriving from London. A later owner of the building is mostly responsible for a story which is still current in Exeter and which has muddied its history; he helped create the myth that Sir Francis Drake and Sir Walter Raleigh planned their strategy against the Armada in 1596 while in the building drinking coffee.

It should have been self-evident that the tale was fanciful given the year (taken from a date on the building) was eight years after the Armada, that Drake had died by then and Raleigh was either in the Tower of London or travelling abroad, and that coffee took another two generations to become popular in England.

What has been forgotten are some salient points about the building. One of these is that for a short while it was the Custom House into which many notable seafarers no doubt did pass. Neither Drake nor Raleigh, however, spent much time in Exeter as adults and certainly were not in the city during the Armada. Of greater relevance, has been the neglect of its history involving women.

In the mid 1720s one Mary Wildy began Mol's and she was followed by Margaret Wildier, Mrs Vinnicombe, Mary Murch, Sarah Hurd, Mary Commins and finally Mary Anne Crosse. The last two women operated the business from another building. In effect, for more than one hundred years the most popular and successful coffee house in the city was run by women.

It was suggested in 1806 that the founder was an Italian man named Mol 'who doubtless found his way to Exeter during the palmy days of the woollen trade'. More than a century later the great W. G. Hoskins thought he was named Thomas Mol and connected him with the building in 1596. Hoskins was, however, wrong in his use of these documents and he was inaccurate in seeing the business as an Elizabethan coffee house. Although no evidence has been found to support the premise, it could be that Mol was a nickname for the first owner, Mary Wildy.

What is intriguing is that the history of Mol's, one of Exeter's most famous buildings, has lain unsuspected for generations. In it we have an example of a successful women-run business that is more interesting than the fabrications of Raleigh and Drake that were crafted to satisfy Victorian tourists.[36]

Wilmot and Thomasin Moreman of Exmoor, two Georgian scolds by Andrew Brice of Exeter

What makes Wilmot Moreman and her sister Thomasin remarkable is partly their use of language. It has been studied as an example of Devon dialect for several centuries. But it is also noteworthy because the two were characters created by a man in the 1720s as a caricature of local working class rural women. While their dialogue is valuable as dialect the portrayal of the two women is less than flattering if not misogynistic.

The authorship remains doubtful. It claims to be the work of Peter Lock, a blind itinerant fiddler of North Molton. Various other suggestions have been put forward for more than a hundred years[37] but it is most likely to have been written by Andrew Brice, Exeter's foremost newspaperman of the early eighteenth century. He called it 'An Exmoor Scolding' and originally published it in his *Weekly Journal* in 1727 at the time Mol's was being established.[38]

In the nearly three hundred years since it first appeared 'An Exmoor Scolding' has continually been reprinted.[39] The two women begin arguing while spinning wool and it is not until their mother orders them to stop does the dialogue finish. Part of the popular appeal has been in their use of outdated language: words such as slammerkin and slattern (a woman slovenly in her habits), rubbacrock ('a filthy slattern that is as black as if she were continually rubbing herself against a boiler or kettle'), swash bucket ('a wench who carelessly

Andrew Brice in 1730

swashes and splashes the pig's wash out of the bucket'), trapes (a slovenly female), trub (a slut) and meazle (sows or swine) are colourful enough to have delighted readers for nearly three centuries. The continual insults have heightened the enjoyment.

The portrayal originates in the longstanding tradition of verbal abuse between women. Brice, if indeed he was the author, lived a short distance from the archive of the diocese and might have known of the large collection of documents which show how similar arguments had been recorded for generations. Included in this mass of material is a record from 1625 when Mary Eller of Southleigh said of Jane Burrowes of the same place 'Thou art a whore, a common whore, and a hedge whore, and a stray mare'.[40] Likewise, that year John Hole of Clannaborough said of Alice Reynolds of Nymet Tracey 'Thou art a whore, an old rotten whore for thirty years ago, a pockey whore & an old rotten witch and a scurvy pated whore'.[41] One of the more outrageous recorded accusations was made by Agnes Ellis of Crediton to her neighbour Christian Brooke in 1629: 'Thou art a whore and my husband's whore and I came and found my husband dealing with thee and thou heldest up thy smock with thine teeth'.[42]

These documents, and many more, were part of legal cases

brought forward by Devonians, nearly all women but there were some exceptions, who considered their good names to have been compromised in the early 1600s. They brought neighbours, former friends or enemies to the church courts in protest and in the hope of clearing their reputations.[43] The collection was greatly damaged, and partially destroyed, by enemy bombing during the Second World War.

The dispute penned between two imaginary Exmoor women could be seen as part of a long history of defamation or equally it could be considered as a male portrayal of working class women from the countryside. Brice was a notable figure in Exeter. He was pursued for publishing the proceedings of the House of Commons, wrote several interesting poems and published two books. Of greater interest in regards to women's history was he employed women as printers: the *Universal Magazine* claimed that more were trained in his office than in virtually any other part of the country. This may also have been due to his daughter Sarah with whom he went into partnership in 1743.[44]

The dialogue begins with a comment from Thomasin to her sister Wilmot. The original text has been supplemented by a translation into Standard English which was published in 1795. It follows the speech of each woman.

Thomasin   Lock! Wilmot, vor why vor did'st roily zo upon ma up
            to Challacomb Row? Ees dedent thenk tha had'st a be
            zich a Labbo' tha Tongue. What a Vengeance! wart
            betwatled, or wart tha baggaged; or had'st tha took a
            Shord, or a paddled?

ALACK, WILMOT, WHEREFORE DID THOUS'T RAIL SO AGAINST ME UP TO CHALLACOMBE REVEL? I DID NOT THINK THOU HAD'ST BEEN SUCH A BLAB. IN THE NAME OF VENGEANCE! WEREN'T BEFOOLED OR BEWITCHED; OR HAD'ST THOU TAKEN A CUP OR GOT FUDDLED?

Wilmot   I roily upon tha, ya gurt, thonging, banging, muxy Drawbreech? Noa, 'twas thee roil'st upon me up to Doraty Vogwill's Upzitting, whan tha vung'st, (and to be hang'd to tha!) to Rabbin. Shou'd zem tha wart zeck arter Me-at and Me-al. And zo tha merst, by ort es know, wey guttering; as gutter tha wutt whan tha com'st to good tackling. But some zed "Shoor and shoor tha did'st bet make wise, to zee nif tha young Josy Heaff-field wou'd come to zlack thy boddize, and whare a wou'd be O vore or no." Bet 'twas thy old disyease, Chun.

I RAIL AGAINST THEE, YOU GREAT, LONGING, UNWIELDY, DIRTY DRAGGLE-TAIL? NO, THOU RAIL'ST AGAINST ME AT DOROTHY FOGWELL'S CHRISTENING FEAST, WHEN THOU STOOD'ST GODMOTHER (HANG THEE!) TO ROBIN. IT SEEMS THOU WERT SICK AFTER MEALS – AND SO THOU MIGHTST, FOR AUGHT I KNOW, WITH GUTTLING; FOR GUTTLE THOU WILT WHEN THOU COMEST TO GOOD VICTUALS. BUT SOME SAID *TRULY THOU DIDST BUT COUNTERFEIT TO TRY WHETHER THE YOUNG JOSEPH HEATHFIELD WOULD COME TO SLACKEN THEY STAYS AND WHETHER HE WOULD BE ANXIOUS ABOUT THEE OR NOT.* BUT TWAS THE OLD DISEASE, QUEEN.

Thomasin   Hey go! What disyease dest me-an, ya gurt dugged-teal'd, swapping, rousling Blowze? Ya gurt Roile, tell ma. Tell ma, a zey, what disyease dest me-an? Ad! chell ream my heart, to tha avore Ise let tha lipped. — Chell tack et out wi' tha to tha true Ben, fath! Tell ma, a zey, what disyease dest me-an that tha zest cham a troubled wey?

HEYDEY! WHAT DISEASE DOST MEAN, YOU GREAT DRAGGLE-TAILED, CLUMSY, RUSTLING SLAMMERKIN? YOU GREAT HOYDEN, TELL ME. TELL ME, I SAY, WHAT DISEASE DOST MEAN? EGAD! I'LL SPLIT MY LUNGS, BEFORE I LET THEE

REST. I'LL SCOLD IT OUT WITH THEE TO THE PURPOSE, SAITH. TELLME, I SAY, WHAT DISEASE DOTH MEAN, THAT HOUSAYST I'M TROUBLED WITH?

Wilmot   Why; ya purting, tatchy, stertling, jowering, prinking, mincing theng, chell tell tha what disyease. Is dedn't me-an the Boneshave, ner the Heartgun, ner the Allernbatch that tha had'st in thy Niddiok. 'Tes better twar: vor than Ount Annis Moreman coul'd ha' blessed vore, and net ha' pomster'd about et, as Moather ded.

WHY, YOU POUTING, TOUCHY, WRIGGLING, BRAWLING, PROUD MINX, I'LL TELL THEE WHAT DISEASE. I DID NOT MEAN THE RHEUMATISM, NOR THE HYSTERICS, NOR THE OLD BOILS THAT THOU HAD'ST IN THEY NECK. IT WERE BETTER SO, FOR THEN AUNT ANNIS MOREMAN COULD HAVE MADE A CHARM FOR IT, AND NOT HAVE USED SO MANY SLAPS AND SALVES ABOUT IT AS MOTHER DID.

Thomasin   What disyease than, ya gurt haggage?

WHAT DISEASE THEN, YOU GREAT SLOVEN?

Wilmot   Why, e'er zince tha wart twanty, zewnteen and avore, tha hast a be' troubled wey the Doul vetch tha.

WHY, EVER SINCE THOU WERT TWENTY, AYE SEVENTEEN, AND BEFORE, THOU HAST BEEN TROUBLED WITH THE DEVIL-TAKE-THEE.

Thomasin   What's me-an by that, ya long-hanjed Meazel? Dist hire ma? Tha call'st ma stertling roil now-reert. — How dedst thee stertlee upon the zess last harvest wey the young Dick Vrogwill, whan George Vuzz putch'd? He told ma the whole fump o' th' besneze.

WHAT DO YOU MEAN BY THAT, YOU LONG-GUTTED SOW? DOST THOU HEAR ME? THOU CALLED'ST ME WRIGGLING HAYDEN JUST NOW. HOW DIDST THOU WRIGGLE UPON THE MOW LAST HARVEST WITH THE YOUNG DICK FROGWELL, WHEN GEORGE FURSE STACKED THE HAY! HE TOLD ME EVERY CIRCUMSTANCE OF THE AFFAIR.

Wilmot   O! the very vengeance tear tha! Dest thee tell me o' Dick Vrogwill? why thee art in a ninniwatch e'ery other torn, nif zo be tha dest bet zet zeert in Harry Vursdon.

OH! VENGEANCE TAKE THEE! DOST THOU TELL ME OF DICK FROGWELL? WHY THOU ART IN A FOOL'S ANXIETY EVERY NOW AND THEN IF THOU DOST BUT GET A SIGHT OF HENRY FURSDON.

Thomasin   How! ya gurt chonnting, grumbling, glumping, zower-zapped, yerring trash!

HOW! YOU GREAT TAUNTING, GRUMBLING, SULKY, CRABBED, YELLING SLUT!

Wilmot   Don't tell me o' glumping: oil the neighbourhooden knowth thee to be a veaking, blazing, tiltish hussey.

DON'T TELL ME OF SULLENESS; ALL THE NEIGHBOURHOOD KNOWS THEE TO BE A FRETFUL, BACKBITING, TESTY HUSSY.

Thomasin   And thee art a crewnting, querking, yeavy, dugged-yess, chockling baggage.

AND THOU ART A GAUNTING, BROKEN-WINDED, HEAVY, DRAGGLED-TAIL, HECTORING BAGGAGE.

Wilmot   Net zo chockling, ner it zo crewnting, as thee art, a colting hobby-horse! Nif tha dest bet go down into the paddick, to stroak the kee, thee wut come oll a gerred, and oll horry zo vurs tha art a vorked ; ya gerred-teal'd, panking, hewstring meazel! Thee art a skittish Sture jest a yooked. Tha ouldst bost any keendest theng, tha are so vore-reet, nif Vauther dedn't ha-ape tha.

NOT SO HECTORING, NOR YET SO GRUNTING, AS THOU ART, A ROMPING HOBBY HORSE! IF THOU DOST BUT GO DOWN INTO THE PARK, TO MILK THE COWS, THOU WILL COME HOME ALL BEMIRED, AND ALL DAUBED, AS HIGH AS THOU ART FORKED; YOU DIRTY-TAILED, PANTING, WHEEZ-ING SOW! THOU ART LIKE A GIDDY STEER JUST YOKED. THOU WOULDST BREAK EVERY SORT OF UTENSIL, THOU ART SO HEEDLESS, IF FATHER DID NOT CHEEK THEE.

Thomasin   Ay, ay! Kester Moreman wou'd ha be hove up, nif zo be a had a had tha; a toteling, wambling, zlottering, zart-and-vair yheatstool.

AYE, AYE! CHRISTOPHER MOREMAN WOULD HAVE BEEN RARELY OFF, IF HE HAD HAD THEE, A LOITERING, LOLLING, SLOPPING SICKLY IDLER.

Wilmot   Ay, and zo wou'd tha young George Vuzz, mun, whan a had a had a rubbacrock, rouzeabout, platvooted, zidlemovith'd swashbucket. Pitha dest thenk enny theng will e'er vittee or gooddee wey zich a what-nozed, haggle-tooth'd, stare-bason, timersome, rixy, wapper-e'ed theng as thee art?

AYE, AND SO WOULD THE YOUNG GEORGE FURSE, WOMEN, WHEN HE HAD GOT A SLUTTISH, RESTLESS, SPLAY-FOOT-ED, WRY-MOUTHED SLATTERN. PRITHEE, DOST THINK

ANYTHING WILL GO WELL OR PROSPER WITH SUCH A RED-NOSED, HAGGLE-TOOTHED, BARE-FACED, HEAD-STRONG, QUARRELSOME, GOGGLE-EYED THING AS THOU ART?

Thomasin   Dest hire ma? Oll the crime o' the country goth, that wan tha liv'st up to tha cot, tha wert the old Rager Hill's under bed-blonket. And more 'an zo, that tha wert a chittcring, raving, racing, bozzom-chucked, rigging, lonching, haggaging Moil.

DOST HEAR ME? ALL THE REPORT OF THE COUNTRY IS,T HAT WHEN THOU LIVEST UP AT THE COTTAGE, THOU WERT THE OLD ROGER HILL'S UNDER BED BLANKET. AND, MOREOVER, THAT THOU WERT A TATTLING, BACK-BITING, BLUBBER-CHEEKED, WANTON, STRADDLING, SLOVENLY MULE.

Wilmot   How! ya confounded Trapes! Tell me enny more o' Rager Hill's Bed-Blonket, ad! cheel pull the Poll o' tha; chell plim tha, chell vulch tha. Looks zee, Rager Hill es as hones a Man as enny in Challacomb; no dispreise.

HOW! YOU CONFOUNDED TRAPES! TELL ME ANY MORE OF BEING ROGER HILL'S BED BLANKET, EGAD! I'LL PULL THY POLL; I'LL THRASH THEE, I'LL THUMP THEE. DO YOU SEE – ROGER HILL IS AS HONEST A MAN AS ANY IN CHALLACOMB; AND NO DISPARAGEMENT TO ANY BY THE COMPARISON.

Thomasin   And do thee tell me o' sterlting upon thee Zess, whan George Vuzz putch'd, chell gi' tha a lick; chell lay tha over the years wey the Vire-Tangs. Ad! chell-ting tha. Thy buzzom chucks were pretty vittee avore tha mad'st thyzel therle, and thy vlesh oll wangery, and thy skin oll vlagged, with nort bet agging, and veaking, and tiltishness.

AND DO THOU TELL ME OF WRIGGLING UPON THE MOW, WHEN GEORGE FURZE PITCHED, I'LL BELAY THEE OVER THE EARS WITH THE FIRE-TONGS. EGAD! I'LL TINGLE THEE. THY BLOWSY CHEEKS WERE PRETTY HEALTHY BEFORE THOU MADEST THYSELF LANK AND THEY FLESH ALL FLABBY, THY SKIN ALL WRINKLED, WITH NOTHING BUT SNARLING, AND FRETTING AND TESTINESS.

Wilmot   Bed-blonket akether! Ha! zey zich a word more chell cotton thy waistecoat. Chell thong tha, chell gi' tha zich a strat in tha chups, ya grizzledemundy.

BED-BLANKET QUOTE HER! HA! SAY SUCH A WORD AGAIN, I'LL COTTON THY WAISTCOAT. I'LL SLOG THEE, I'LL GIVE THEE SUCH A SLAP IN THE FACE, YOU SNEERING FOOL.

Thomasin   Me a strat in the chups? Dest hire ma? Come aneest me, chell pummel tha chell vag tha, lace tha.

ME A SLAP IN THE FACE? DOST HEAR ME? COME NEAR ME, I'LL BOX THEE, I'LL FAT THEE, I'LL LACE THEE.

Wilmot   Thee lace ma? Chem a laced well-a-fine aready. Zey wone word more, and chell bresh tha, chell tan tha, chell make thy boddize pilmee.

THEE LACE ME? I'M LACED WELL ENOUGH ALREADY. SAY ONE WORD MORE, AND I'LL BRUSH THEE, I'LL THAN THEE, I'LL THRESH THE DUST OUT OF THEY STAYS.

Thomasin   How a man a zed! Make my boddize pilmee? Ad! if e'er tha squeakest wone word more o' tha bed-blonket, chell trim tha, chell crown tha, chell vump tha.

HOW A MANLY THREAT INDEED? THRESH THE DUST OUT OF MY STAYS! EGAD! IF EVER THOU SQUEAKEST ONE WORD

MORE OF THE BED-BLANKET, I'LL TRIM THEE, I'LL BREAK THY HEAD, I'LL THUMP THEE.

Wilmot   Why dedst thee, than, tell me o' the Zess, or et of the Hay-pook, as tha dedst whileer? Chell drub tha, chell curry thy scabbed yess var tha.

WHY DID'ST THOU TELL ME OF THE MOW, OR YET OF THE HAY STACK, AS THOU DID'ST AWHILE SINCE? I'LL DRUB THEE, I'LL SCRUB TH Y SCABBED ARSE FOR THEE.

Thomasin   And why dest thee, than tell me 'ilsterday o' losing my rewden hat in the rex- Bush out whorting? And more 'an zo, that the young Tom Vuzz shou'd leave he's cod-glove! Ad! zey a word more o' the young Tom Vuzz, chell baste tha, chell stram tha, chell drash tha; chell make thy kopp hoppee, wi' thy Vlanders lace upon't.

AND WHY DID'ST THOU, THEN, TELL ME YESTERDAY OF LOSING MY STRAW HAT IN THE RUSHES, WHEN OUT GATHERING OF WORTS? AND, MOREOVER, THAT THE YOUNG TOM FURSE SHOULD LEAVE HIS HEDGING GLOVE? EGAD! SAY ONE WORD MORE OF THE YOUNG TOM FURSE, I'LL SCRAM THEE, I'LL THRESH THEE, I'LL MAKE THY CAP HOP, WITH THY FLANDERS LACE UPON IT.

Wilmot   Vlanders lace! What's me-an by that, ha-ah? Tell me enny more o' Vlanders lace, chell make thy yead addle. Chell up wi' ma veest, and gi' tha a wisterpoop, and zitch a zwop as shall make tha veel ma, looks zee!

FLANDERS LACE! WHAT DOST MEAN BY THAT? TELL ME AGAIN OF FLANDERS LACE! I'LL MAKE THEY HEAD ADDLE. I'LL UP WITH MY FIST, AND GIVE THEE A BOX ON THE EAR, AND SUCH A BOUNCE AS SHALL MAKE THEE FEEL ME, MARK MY WORD!

Thomasin   Gi' me a zwop? Ad! chell gi' tha a wherret, or a zlat in
            the chups, or up wi' thy dugged coats, and tack tha
            gre-asy yess o' tha.

GIVE ME A BOUNC? EGAD! I'LL GIVE THEE A BOX ON THE EAR,
OR A SLAP IN THE CHOPS, OR UP WITH THEY DRAGGLED
COATS, AND SLAP THE GREASY ARSE OF THEE.

Wilmot   Thee tack ma, ya unlifty, ill-hearty, untidy meazle?
            Andra wou'd ha' had a Trub in tha, nif Vauther hadent
            a strat the match.

THOU SLAP ME YOU UNWIELDY, ILL-NATURED, SLOVENLY
SOW? ANDREW WOULD HAVE HAD A TROLL IN THEE, IF
FATHER HAD NOT BROKE OFF THE MATCH.

Thomasin   How dem! a trub? Go, ye rearing, snapping, tedious,
            cutted snibblenose! Th' art olways a vustled up in an
            old jump, or a whittle, or an old seggard, avore zitch
            times as Neckle Halse comath about: Than tha wut
            prinkee. Thee hast a let the kee go zoo vor want o'
            strocking. It a vore oll th'art an abomination pinchvart
            vor thy own eends. Ay, ay! Shoort, Wilmot, shoort!
            Zwer thy torn, or else tha tedst net carry whome thy
            pad, and meet Neckle Halse by tha wey. He'll meet tha
            in the Vuzzy-park coander by cockleert, or avore, chell
            warndy.

HOW, YOU SLUT! A TROLL? GO, YOU MOCKING, INAPPING,
TEDIOUS, MISERY SNIVELLER! THOU ART ALWAYS WRAPPED
UP IN AN OLD PAIR OF STAYS OR A CLOAK OR AN OLD
SAFEGUARD, TILL SUCH TIMES AS NICHOLAS HALSE COMES
ABOUT. THEN THOU WILT PRINK. THOU HAST LET THE
COWS GO DRY FOR WANT OF MILKING. YET, NEVERTHELESS,
THOU ART A CURSED NIGGARD FOR THY OWN ENDS. AYE,
AYE, WORK, WILMOT WORK! TWIRL THY SPINNING TURN,

OR ELSE THOU WILT NOT CARRY HOME THY PAD AND MEET NICHOLAS HALSE BY THE WAY. HE'LL MEET THEE IN THE FURZY PARK CORNER BY TWILIGHT OR BEFORE I'LL WARRANT YOU.

Wilmot   Tell ma wone word more o' Neckle Halse, chell skull tha, tha hassent a be' a skull'd zo vor wone while. Ya gurt fustilugs! The old Mag Dawkins es bet a Huckmuck to tha. Zet tha about ort, why, tha dest thengs vore-and-back, a cat-hamm'd, a vore-reert, and vrarap-shapen, like a totle.

TELL ME ONE WORD MORE OFNICHOLAS HALSE, I'LL SCOLD THEE, THOU HAST NOT BEEN SO SCOLDED FOR A LONG WHILE. YOU GREAT RAW-BONED CREATURE. OLD MARGERY DAWKINS IS BUT A DWARF TO THEE. SET THEE ABOUT ANY THING , WHY THOU DOST IT AWKWARDLY, FUMBLING, HEADSTRONGLY AND CLUMSILY LIKE A FOOL.

Thomasin   How! ya long-hanged Trapes! Ya blow-monger baarge! Thee wut coal-varty a-bed avore be voor days. Th'art so deeve as a Haddick in chongy weather. Or whan 'tes avrore or a scratcht the le-ast theng out, or whan snewth, or blunketh, or doveth, or in scatty weather, or in a tingling vrost, than tha art theck-listed, and ba hang'd to tha.

HOW! YOU LONG-GUTTED TROLLOP! YOU OVER-FED HOG! THOU WILT WARM THE BED WITH FARTING BEFORE DAYBREAK. THOU ART AS DEAF AS A HADDOCK IN CHANGEABLE WEATHER. OR WHEN TIS FROSTY, OR A LEAST ICE APPEARS, OR WHEN IT SNOWS, OR SLEETS, OR THAWS, OR IN SHOWERY WEATHER, OR IN SHARP FROST, THEN THOU ARE SHORT-BREATHED, HANG THEE!

Wilmot   And thee art a lams'd in wone o'thy yearms, and
          cassent zee a sheen in thy reart ee.

AND THOU ART LAMED IN ONE ARM, AND CAN'ST NOT SEE
A RAY OF LIGHT IN THY RIGHT EYE.

Thomasin   Rex-bush! Fath! tell me o' tha rex-bush, ye tee-heeing
           pixy! Es marl who's more vor rigging, or rumping,
           steehopping or ragrowtering, giggleting or gambowling
           than thee art thyzel. Pitha, dest'nt remember whan
           tha com'st over tha clam wi' tha old Hugh Hosegood,
           whan tha wawter was by stave, how tha vel'st in, and
           the old Hugh drade thee out by tha vorked eend, wi'
           thy dugged clathers up zo vur as thy na'el, whan tha
           wart just a buddled?

RUSHES! FAITH! TELL ME THE RUSHES YOU TITTERING
ELF. I WONDER WHO IS MORE FOR WANTONING OR
ROMPING, CAPERING, CLOTHES-RUMPLING, GIGGLETING
OR GAMBOLING THAN THOU ART THYSELF. PRITHEE,
DOST NOT REMEMBER WHEN THOU COMEST ACROSS THE
NARROW PLANK BRIDGE WITH THE OLD HUGH HOSEGOOD,
WHEN THE WATER WAS AS HIGH AS THE BOARD, HOW THOU
TUMBLEST IN, AND THE OLD HUGH DREW THEE OUT BY THE
LEGS, WITH THY DIRTY CLOTHES AS HIGH AS THY NAVEL,
WHEN THOU WERT ALMOST DROWNED.

Wilmot   Lock! dest dwallee, or tell doil? Pitha tell reaznable, or
          hold thy popping, ya gurt washamouth.

LACK A DAY! DOST THOU SPEAK DELIRIOUSLY, OR TALK
WILDLY? PRITHEE, TALK REASONABLY OR HOLD THY
GABBLE, YOU GREAT BLABBER.

This was the end of the first half, entitled the 'first bout'. It ends with Wilmot pulling her sister's poll (cap). She cries murder to her mother who stops the argument.

How rural women in Devon would have responded to this portrayal will never be known. Perhaps it would have been enjoyed for its comic qualities. What is certain is that through nearly three centuries this remarkable dialogue has continued to find a new audience.

Miss Anne Hamilton of late Georgian Exeter, a 'gentlewoman of the old school'

Wilmot and Thomasine Moreman had little in common with Mrs Anne McTaggart who, in 1830, when she was in her late seventies, looked back upon her life and wrote *Memoirs of a Gentlewoman of the Old School*. For those interested in Devon her account is fascinating for what she says of Exeter in the early 1770s when she was Miss Anne Hamilton, then a young woman in her late teens. Unhappy family circumstances had necessitated she was sent from her home in Tiverton to Exeter where she was in the care of her widowed uncle. There she lived in his large house in the High Street and had a very comfortable lifestyle. For three years she was his guest and appears to have spent her days in agreeable leisure and luxury.

Her book is addressed to a younger, female audience. She explains that at that time there were several regiments in Exeter which helped to enhance the city's social life by providing musical bands for balls. She notes that in her youth young women danced from seven in the evening until four or five in the morning with only bread and butter, biscuits and negus (a hot drink made of wine, water, sugar and spices) to fortify them. Unlike Regency England they did not, she explained to 'my dear young readers', have savoury viands and strong drinks.

In her first months, during winter, she spent her very early mornings at the 6.15 service at the cathedral. At that time, she wrote, it attracted only a few elderly people and she walked to the cathedral in inclement weather with a friend under what she claimed was the only umbrella in Exeter. This had been imported by her uncle from Portugal.

Her enthusiasm for church-going waned and was replaced by a love of plays and balls. Oddly, in her account she challenged 'bible-readers' to find a biblical passage which forbids either. Her modesty would not allow her to attend either the first or last ball of the season. This was intended to signify she was neither too eager to begin dancing nor unwilling to give it up.

In addition to official balls, she belonged to a group of young women, or young ladies as she termed them, who met one evening a week to work and read approved books and then dance for an hour. As they had no music they sang. In respect to the books Hamilton criticized the younger generation for 'thinking better of their own judgement' than that of their parents. It was 'a sad mistake in general'. For this she blamed Mary Wollstonecraft, the author of *A Vindication of the Rights of Woman* which was not published until 1792. It was perhaps because Wollstonecraft had argued for the education of women that Hamilton objected but it was probably as much due to her own innate conservatism.

Hamilton also wrote with distaste of the popular celebrations in Exeter which followed the release from prison of John Wilkes, the radical who advocated for the freedom of the press. Perhaps it was not surprising given that a mob had paraded down the High Street and upon seeing her uncle's house in darkness, an indication of disapproval of Wilkes, they proceeded to break his windows.

Anne Hamilton was no doubt similar to many other young women of her station who then lived in other country towns across the country. But what distinguished her for Devon are the insights into a few years of the otherwise poorly-recorded genteel social life of Exeter.[45]

Maria Foote of Plymouth, and Countess of Harrington

It is likely that Mrs McTaggart would not have approved of Maria Foote who transformed herself from being the pitied daughter of a theatrical family to becoming part of the aristocracy. She was born at Plymouth in 1797, the daughter of Samuel T. Foote, a theatre manager, and his wife, a Miss Hannington. Twenty-eight years later, in 1825, she was at the heart of a national scandal and one newspaper columnist wrote 'if there was ever a creature who merited the sympathy of the world it is Maria Foote'. The blame, in his opinion, lay with the ladies of Plymouth who treated her parents badly. Her mother was 17 when she married Samuel T. Foote twenty-five years her senior.[46] He later moved to Exeter where he ran the Royal Clarence Hotel.[47]

'In country towns actors are considered profligate people and though the young creature had been educated as a lady and was much more of one than most of the other females in the town, no genteel family paid her the least attention. She was considered the wife of a man whom nobody respected and notwithstanding the whole town was interested in her appearance, pity was the predominant feeling whenever she appeared.'

Maria Foote in 1824

Maria Foote, 'she was but a foot yesterday, but she is higher now' at her marriage

41

Maria Foote as Maria Darlington, 1822

The marriage was unhappy and eventually Mrs Foote became an actress at her husband's theatre. Then their daughter Maria was put on stage, at the age of 12, playing Juliet to her mother's Romeo.

> 'The town was disgusted – thoroughly disgusted – and whatever claims he had before to the notice of some private friends, to whom his manners as a gentleman ever made him welcome, they were now considered forfeited forever'.[48]

Four years later, in 1814, Maria, now 'fascinating and amiable',[49] made her début at Covent Garden and appeared there in every season until 1825. The following year she was at Drury Lane but she also toured extensively throughout the country and received great acclaim, particularly for her beauty. The great Shakespearian William Macready wrote on one occasion 'the lovely Miss Foote . . . produced the most pleasing effect by aiming at none'.[50] She herself is credited with having admitted 'I was never a great actress, though people thought me fascinating, and that I suppose I was'.[51]

In 1815 she became the mistress of Colonel William Berkeley, later Earl Fitzhardinge. They had two children but he broke a promise of marriage. In 1824 she ended their relationship and received an offer of marriage from Joseph Hayne, known as 'Pea-green' because of the colour of his coat. He also withdrew the marriage offer but she successfully sued for breach of promise in 1824 and received £3,000 in damages. It was this scandal which prompted the journalist's recollection of her early life.

Miss Foote returned to Covent Garden and on her first night 'was received with a burst of loud, continued and enthusiastic acclamation such as we never remember to have heard or known to have been equalled at any theatre'.[52] She last performed on stage in 1831 and married Charles Stanhope, fourth earl of Harrington. He was then 51 and she was aged 33. She died in 1867 having been largely ignored by high society.[53] After her death it was recollected that in London the Countess maintained the style of transport as used by her late husband; there were 'large black horses, with the square blinkers and the brass-mounted harness, drawing the stately-looking carriage in which the Countess was seated. The servants invariably wore chocolate-coloured coats reaching to their heels'.[54] Just after she died one columnist wrote she 'began life as a pretty actress and took the town by storm, one is afraid to say how many years ago. It would hardly be desirable to recall all the incidents of her earlier life, some of which gained for her a notoriety that had nothing to do with her fame as an actress. It is pleasant to remember that during her later days she gained an extended reputation for her silent works of charity'.[55]

Mary Anne Burges of Awliscombe

Mary Anne Burges of Awliscombe near Honiton is largely a forgotten figure in Devon's past although she was remarkable in the life she carved out for herself amongst Devon's literary figures in the late eighteenth and early nineteenth centuries. Her home was Tracey, a large country house which has recently been demolished. She was born in Edinburgh in 1763. Burges was a linguist (French and Spanish and studied Italian, Dutch and Turkish) and published *The Progress of the Pilgrim Good Intent in Jacobinical Times* which from 1800 to 1822 went into three editions in the United States, three editions in Ireland and ten editions in England.

Burges was also a noted botanist who was consulted by a number of writers for her knowledge of Devon's flora and fauna. For example, Reverend John Swete, the self-avowed Devon expert on the Picturesque Movement, noted her 'elegant accomplishments are the least of her merits' while the Reverend Polwhele thought her 'classical taste and knowledge of botany and ornithology are accompanied with all the diffidence of an ingenious mind'.[56] When Jean Andre Deluc, the reader to Queen Charlotte, was making his geological tour of Devon in 1806, he stayed with Miss Burges.[57] Three years earlier a Scottish visitor, Mrs Grant, the wife of a minister from Inverness-shire, thought she was 'very learned but extremely odd. To describe her is impossible and to me tis impossible to judge whether her peculiarity of manner is the result of affectation or some odd habit'.[58]

Miss Burges made her mark when she was still single. Her greatest

A self portrait of Miss Burges, 1790s

contribution to Devon studies lies in the extraordinary lengthy correspondence she had with her great friend, Mrs Elizabeth Simcoe, the wife of the Governor General of Canada. Mrs Simcoe was a neighbour and Burges' greatest friend. She was twenty-eight when she began writing the letters.

Devoted letters were sent, sometimes several in a week, from 1791 to 1796. In them she declared her undying friendship and gives accounts of her daily life and local news and gossip of Devon. On one occasion she had a holiday in Dartmouth of which she wrote:

'I have been spending the two last days very pleasantly; the weather has been delightful & I have been a great deal out to enjoy it. Yesterday I made quite a voyage on the river. I went on board several vessels; among others a Dutch Galliot, where I saw all the Dutch people at dinner

A woman admired by Miss Burges, 1790s

& was much diverted with their figures & conversations, though I understood little of the latter.'

In many of the letters there is information of Mrs Simcoe's children. In one passage she wrote news which Mrs Simcoe, three thousand miles away, was probably longing to hear:

'Children are all quite well & seem very happy. The elder ones much regret your absence, but I do not think they have any other subject of disquietude, unless indeed it is the multiplication table, of which they are at present very deeply involved in the study. Eliza makes great progress in French. I heard her translating yesterday, & was surprised how little assistance she required. She has a great friendship with Mrs Hunt, who takes more part in instructing her than the others. The only thing I see about her of which you would disapprove, is that they have made her some jackets; but her figure looks so nice in them, that I think it

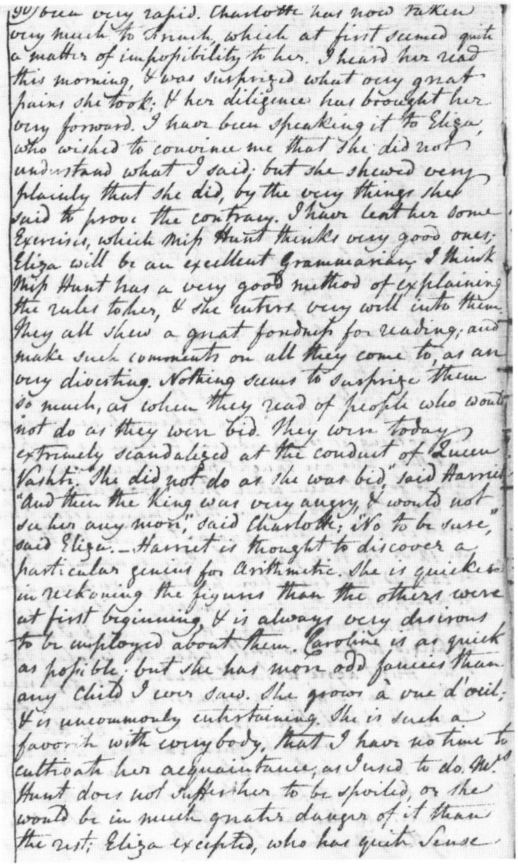

One of the letters from Miss Burges to Mrs Simcoe

[handwritten letter]

yo/been very rapid. Charlotte has now taken
very much to French, which at first seemed quite
a matter of impossibility to her. I heard her read
this morning, & was surprized what very great
pains she took; & her diligence has brought her
very forward. I have been speaking it to Eliza,
who wished to convince me that she did not
understand what I said; but she shewed very
plainly that she did, by the very things she
said to prove the contrary. I have lent her some
Exercises, which Miss Hunt thinks very good ones;
Eliza will be an excellent Grammarian I think
Miss Hunt has a very good method of explaining
the rules to her, & she enters very well into them
They all shew a great fondness for reading; and
make such comments on all they come to, as are
very diverting. Nothing seems to surprize them
so much, as when they read of people who would
not do as they were bid. They were today
extremely scandalized at the conduct of Queen
Vashti. She did not do as she was bid, said Harriet
"And then the King was very angry, & would not
see her any more," said Charlotte; "No to be sure,"
said Eliza.—Harriet is thought to discover a
particular genius for Arithmetic. She is quicker
in reckoning the figures than the others were
at first beginning, & is always very desirous
to be employed about them. Caroline is as quick
as possible; but she has more odd fancies than
any child I ever saw. She grows à une d'oeil;
& is uncommonly entertaining. She is such a
favorite with everybody, that I have no time to
cultivate her acquaintance, as I used to do. Mrs
Hunt does not suffer her to be spoiled, or she
would be in much greater danger of it than
the rest; Eliza excepted, who has great sense.

would reconcile you to the dress, notwithstanding all your aversion to it. I scarce ever saw anybody but her, that did not look either clumsy or pert with a jacket on, but she is as little one as the others, & what I cannot comprehend since it is a dress I never saw you wear, she looks more like you in it, than ever she did before. Charlotte takes great pains in everything she learns. She is particularly improved in dancing, which they practice every day & has almost got rid of that unsteady motion she used to have. Harriett is likewise very diligent, & appears to me to have made an extraordinary progress in reading, in which she seems to take great pleasure. She is grown fatter than she was for some time before you went; & her complexion is in high beauty. Caroline has made the most visible advances. She has now as healthy a look as any of them, joins in all their plays & is generally the merriest of the party. I asked her whether I should say anything for her to you; her answer was "Say, *ma cheri Amie*, & send a kiss".'

It is perhaps because of the continual notes on the children that Mrs Simcoe brought back the letters: in effect these were her lost years as a mother. Other letters concern life in and around Honiton. On one occasion she had an unexpected foreign visitor arrive at her home.

'I should have stayed longer had not my solitude been invaded by the appearance of a Turk, who accosted me in Spanish. This was almost as great an adventure as Don Juan at Torris. He told me his name was Mahomet Basha, & that he was a Turkish Admiral. Had he declared himself to be the Grand Signor in person, the magnificence of his dress would have seemed to confirm the fact. He made me a long visit. He requested to see my husband, when he found no such person existed, he enquired for my father, or for the brother with whom I lived; & when after all his questions he was at last convinced that I really lived by myself, his astonishment was so great, that I doubt whether, at his return to Constantinople, he will think it one of the adventures of his travels more worthy to be related.'

Mary Anne Burges' wealth allowed her an independence to indulge her interests but it was the sharpness of her intellect which made her highly regarded in Devon genteel society. Their importance to the recipient is seen in that the collection of hundreds of letters was brought back with Mrs Simcoe on her return journey to England. Three hundred years later they still form part of the Simcoe family papers.[59] Miss Burges died in 1813 aged 49 and was buried in Awliscombe.[60]

Granny Scott and Betsy Gammon
of Ilfracombe

Not long after Mrs Simcoe returned across the Atlantic a group of Ilfracombe women successfully defended their town from foreign invasion. The story of how they used guile has been told and retold for more than two hundred years. On the 22nd of February 1797 a small French force arrived off Ilfracombe and because there were no men to defend the port local women paraded in their red petticoats to give the French the impression that there were armed men in uniform waiting for an attack. An account appeared in the *Bristol Journal* not long afterwards[61] but the story has been questioned: one Victorian historian of Devon dismissed it with a note 'there is hardly a seaport in Devon that has not some tradition of invaders being scared by a muster of old women in red cloaks'.[62] Others have pointed out that the story is prevalent in Cornwall and Wales.[63] In 1859 Wilkie Collins, the humorist, wrote of the would-be attack in his *The Great (Forgotten) Invasion* but curiously did not mention the involvement of women.

'Of the four ships which the *Directory* had sent to conquer England, two were frigates and two were smaller vessels. This formidable fleet sailed along, in view of a whole panic-stricken, defenceless coast; and the place at which it seemed inclined to try the invading experiment first, was ill-fated Ilfracombe. The commander of the expedition brought his ships up before the harbour, scuttled a few

Granny Scott's drum

coasting-vessels, prepared to destroy the rest, thought
better of it, and suddenly turned his four warlike sterns
on North Devonshire, in the most unaccountable manner.
History is silent as to the cause of this abrupt and
singular change of purpose. Did the chief of the invaders

act from sheer indecision? Did he distrust the hotel accommodation at Ilfracombe? Had he heard of the clotted cream of Devonshire, and did he apprehend the bilious disorganisation of the whole army, if they once got within reach of that rich delicacy? These are important questions, but no satisfactory answer can be found to them. The motives which animated the commander of the invading Frenchmen are buried in oblivion: the fact alone remains, that he spared Ilfracombe. The last that was seen of him from North Devonshire, he was sailing over ruthlessly to the devoted coast of Wales'.[64]

The Commander of the North Devon Militia wrote an interesting letter to the Duke of Portland, then Home Secretary, immediately after the incident and also did not mention women. Lieutenant Colonel Orchard claimed his men gathered to disperse the French but by the time they got to Ilfracombe the invaders had left. He warned this affair 'may be misrepresented and exaggerated'.[65] He appears to be supported by an account the next year entitled *A history of all the real and threatened invasions of England from the landing of Julius Caesar to the present*. That author stated the French had a 'vain attempt' which was thwarted by the North Devon Militia 'assisted by the gentlemen and the peasantry'.[66]

Nevertheless, the involvement of women is given credence by the survival of two objects. In the town museum there is a portion of a red petticoat given by Elizabeth Buckingham in the 1930s. She stated her ancestor had worn that cloth in the ruse in 1797.[67] There is also in Ilfracombe Museum a drum which once belonged to Betsey Gammon who, it is said, used it to rally the women.

These women were not unique in Devon's history in fighting off invaders. In 1404 'the country people' repelled the French at Blackpool, on the road from Slapton to Dartmouth.[68] The battle was a bloody one and part of the credit for the success was attributed to women slinging stones.[69] One of Devon's seventeenth-century writers described them as 'Amazon-like'.[70]

There have been several other occasions when women have

dramatically taken a physical role in Devon's history. They have even been credited with repelling the Vikings at Tiverton: in 1790 Tiverton's most distinguished historian recalled that in 1002 on 'November 13th being St Brice's Day the Danes that were in the town of Tiverton upon the river Isca [Exe] . . . were massacred by the women with much secrecy in the night.'[71] Women have also been said to have attacked the Vikings at Holne on the edge of Dartmoor. According to one tradition, a party of Vikings had sailed up the Dart river and 'a lot of women determined, as the men could not get rid of them, to allow themselves to be taken in a body by the Danes to the castle, and in the night each cut the throat of the man by her'.[72]

Accounts of women fighting men and overcoming them is often about implying weakness in the enemy; writers have often asserted the enemy were not manly enough and were beaten by women. This is also suggested in an account of a skirmish at Tiverton between the council and the poor of the town in 1754. The latter believed they should have the right to elect their members of Parliament and troops were brought in to disperse what became a large crowd. The people were attacked with great violence but, as Tiverton's Georgian historian noted, 'some women seized Lieutenant Suttie by the collar and took away his sword which he never after recovered.' Moreover, it was observed, 'his pride was much hurt by his skirmish with the women and consequent loss of his sword, which disgrace he was frequently reminded of'.[73] Twelve years later there was another popular protest at perceived political corruption in Tiverton and on this occasion a group of local people 'chiefly women, broken into the mayor's house through the windows and into the room where the mayor was and greatly insulted him, pulling off his wig, striking him, twisting his nose, and threatening to kill him if he did not immediately sign a paper they then produced.'[74]

Many of the cases, particularly those involving foreign enemies, cannot be relied upon but what is intriguing with the Ilfracombe women is the survival of two artifacts which by their very existence must make anyone pause in doubting the validity of this Georgian story.

Hannah Cowley, Tiverton's Playwright

At about the time that Granny Scott would have been rallying the women of Ilfracombe Hannah Cowley was ending a successful career as a playwright. She was one of Devon's most successful playwrights and poets. Hannah Cowley was born in Tiverton in 1743, the daughter of Philip and Hannah Parkhouse. Her first play, 'The Runaway' was a great success with Sarah Siddons in the leading role. The subject matter, the injustice of arranged marriages, struck a chord with London audiences particularly the outburst of a female character's on the marriage vow 'to love, honour and obey'; 'I won't hear of it, "love" one might manage that perhaps, but "honour, obey"!, tis strange the ladies had never interest enough to get this ungallant form amended'. A later play, 'Who's the Dupe', also had the theme of arranged marriages: one female character pleads 'The education given to women shuts us entirely from such refined acquaintance'.

Another success was 'The Rivals' in 1775 but from this developed antagonism from Richard Sheridan, the playwright and theatre proprietor, who 'was determined to halt the meteoric rise to fame of this new and wildly popular woman rival'. She then entered, for several years, into a rivalry with Hannah More, a new playwright. Cowley's 'The Belle's Stratagem' opened in 1780 and again explored the lack of wisdom of arranged marriages. It became hugely popular and was performed across the country including throughout Devon.

Cowley continued writing through to the 1790s. In 1883 there was a major restaging of 'The Belle's Strategem' which featured

Ellen Terry. Even so, by 1894 it was claimed that her work had been forgotten. More recently it has been reassessed as fighting for justice for women[75] as well as for its representations of lesbians.[76] She is interesting as Devon's first female playwright and for her custom of opening her house one morning a week to only ladies. She had an aversion to card-playing and dislike of 'the inconvenience of evening amusements'.[77] Mrs Cowley returned to Tiverton after living in London and six years later she died, in 1809, at the age of sixty-six. *The Examiner* wrote she was 'well-known for her bad plays and worse poetry' while the *Morning Chronicle* noted she died 'celebrated throughout society for surely a very high degree of poetic and dramatic genius'.[78]

Hannah Cowley

The Misses Parminters

Very different to Hannah Cowley were two Devon cousins who have given the county a lasting legacy in A-La-Ronde, the eccentric house on the banks of the river Exe; their inspiration was foreign but after two hundred years the result has become firmly part of Devon's heritage. They also created, unusually for Devon as elsewhere in the country, an all-female community.[79] In the 1790s, while Mary Anne Burges was furiously sending off letters across the Atlantic, Hannah Cowley was putting down her pen and the women of Ilfracombe were allegedly defending their homes, two unusual Devon ladies were creating a unique home near Exeter.

The Misses Parminters had North Devon origins. Jane was born in 1750 and the family wealth came from commerce while Mary, who was born seventeen years later, was an orphan who apparently became the ward of Jane's family. In 1784 the two women, along with Jane's sister Elizabeth and a friend, began to tour the continent and they did not finish until eleven years later.[80] The two Misses Parminters then started work on their new home along the river Exe.

The architect is unknown: family tradition claimed it was Jane Parminter. The house is thought to have been based on the chapel of San Vitale in Italy. They named it A la Ronde and its distinctive sixteen sides with interconnecting rooms round a central octagonal hall is one of the most unusual buildings in Devon. The house is equally known for the internal decoration: visitors remember the shells, feathers and stones which abound throughout the house.

Neither cousin married. Religion was a central part of their lives and they were practicing Moravians. Jane died in 1811 and was buried in a vault beneath Point-In-View, the chapel they had built in the grounds. By the chapel are almshouses which were intended for unmarried women, preferably Jews who had converted to Christianity and who were over the age of fifty, and a school for six poor girls who would again hopefully have Jewish parents. A group of oak trees were planted and Jane Parminter left instructions that they were to be left standing until Israel was restored.[81] These trees were later the inspiration for a passerby who began evangelising work among the Jews.[82]

Mary did not die until 1849 and was buried in the same vault as her cousin. Her will stipulated that the estate could only pass to unmarried women in the family. This was later changed and eventually the house was sold to the National Trust.[83] Two hundred years later the essence of their lives' work can still be appreciated.

Joanna Southcott, Gittisham's Prophet

It was also in the 1790s that Joanna Southcott became at once Devon's most famous and yet only prophet. The lack of any competitors does not diminish the impact she made throughout the country from the late 1700s to her death in 1814 and long afterwards. She must rank as one of the most unusual of the women in this collection of remarkable lives.

She was born in 1750 in Taleford near Ottery St Mary and was raised in nearby Gittisham. Her parents were tenant farmers and during her twenties and thirties she worked in a variety of jobs.[84] In Exeter, before Southcott's death, it was recalled she had worked in a local upholsterer's shop some twenty years before.

Joanna Southcott in 1812

'The shopkeeper, being a Methodist, his shop was frequently visited by ministers of the same persuasion, and Joanna Southcott possessing what they termed a *serious turn of mind* did not go unnoticed. She had frequent discussions in the shop and was regarded as a prodigy.'

It was also remembered that in the shop she had a revelation.

'One morning in sweeping out the shop (it is not stated whether or not she had a miraculous broom) she found a seal with the initials J. S., this could not possibly mean any other person than Joanna Southcott. From this moment she bid adieu to the shop and commenced a prophetess.'[85]

Possibly it was her promise to her mother that she would devote her life to one of piety that caused her not to marry. Visions began in 1792 when she was forty-two years old: a voice gave her predictions including of local events. She claimed to have foreknowledge of the death of Bishop Fuller of Exeter in 1796 and of local crop failures. In 1801, at the age of 51, she published *The Strange Effects of Faith; with Remarkable Prophecies (Made in 1792)*. The book brought her public attention and followers. The following year she moved to London and she toured the country. She also issued dozens of pamphlets over the next decade. Many thousands were sold as her followers increased.

Southcott believed that a woman would lead the millennial change: her voice told her 'I will conquer in woman's form'. Afterwards she claimed that she herself would be the mother of the new Messiah whom she named Shiloh. Southcott was then sixty-four and still a virgin.[86] She was ridiculed across the country; one report at the time called her 'an antiquated virgin'.[87] There had been a history of criticism; in 1809, for instance, *The Examiner* called her 'old, vulgar and illiterate' and later the *Universal Magazine* termed her 'the venerable virgin' whom some thought were mad, others foolish and by most a combination of the two. The press sneered at her claims and her followers responded with letters protesting her honesty.[88] In 1814 her followers became convinced of the forthcoming miracle. In the summer it was claimed she was pregnant and she married in November in order to have the child legitimate. However, the following month she died and the autopsy revealed no trace of a baby. Her critics saw it as confirmation of her being a charlatan while some followers believed the child had mystically disappeared.[89]

Four days after her death her supporters gathered to witness her resurrection but were disappointed.[90] Her movement subsequently fragmented but some remained, held together by the 'great box', in which were placed remaining prophecies. It, like her baby, has since disappeared.[91]

Sarah Catherine Martin and
Old Mother Hubbard of Kitley

In the first decade of the nineteenth century *The comic adventures of old Mother Hubbard* was published. It was written and illustrated by Sarah Catherine Martin at Kitley, the country house near Plymouth. The country house was owned by her brother-in-law John Pollexfen Bastard[92] and various stories have been told as to how Martin wrote the rhyme. In one version it was written for her nieces and nephews and in another Bastard suggested to his bored sister-in-law that she write a poem. An original copy of the book at Kitley was inscribed 'to J. P. B. Esquire, MP for the county of Devon, at whose suggestion, and at whose house, these notable sketches were designed, this volume is with all suitable deference dedicated by his humble servant, S. C. M., 1805.'[93] Old Mother Hubbard is thought to be based on Kitley's housekeeper.

The character had existed for many years before Martin's book and her contribution may have been in extending the first existing lines. Five years before her book's publication Old Mother Hubbard was set to music by Dr Samuel Arnold, the celebrated composer.[94] There were many earlier instances of the character[95] from at least as early as 1590 when Edmund Spenser published *Mother Hubbard's Tale*. Nevertheless, when Martin's book was published in 1805 it was already being advertised as a Christmas gift and within a few years it was being performed as a pantomime.[96] Irrespective of whether Sarah Catherine Martin merely extended an existing text, in effect

OLD Mother Hubbard
Went to the cupboard,
To give her poor dog a bone;
But when she came there
The cupboard was bare,
And so the poor dog had none.

Old Mother Hubbard

60

she composed one of the most notable rhymes in English children's literature and certainly the most well-known for Devon.

Old Mother Hubbard
Went to the cupboard,
To give the poor dog a bone:
When she came there,
The cupboard was bare,
And so the poor dog had none.

She went to the baker's
To buy him some bread;
When she came back
The dog was dead!

She went to the undertaker's
To buy him a coffin;
When she came back
The dog was laughing.

She took a clean dish
to get him some tripe;
When she came back
He was smoking his pipe.

She went to the alehouse
To get him some beer;
When she came back
The dog sat in a chair.

She went to the tavern
For white wine and red;
When she came back
The dog stood on his head.

She went to the fruiterer's
To buy him some fruit;
When she came back
He was playing the flute.

OLD MOTHER HUBBARD

AND HER

WONDERFUL DOG

O<small>LD</small> Mother Hubbard
Went to the cupboard,
To give the poor Dog a bone,
But when she came there,
The cupboard was bare,
And so the poor dog got none.

Another view of Old Mother Hubbard

Kitley in 1833

She went to the tailor's
To buy him a coat;
When she came back
He was riding a goat.

She went to the hatter's
To buy him a hat;
When she came back
He was feeding her cat.

She went to the barber's
To buy him a wig
When she came back
He was dancing a jig.

She went to the cobbler's
To buy him some shoes;
When she came back
He was reading the news.

OLD MOTHER HUBBARD
AND HER DOG.

Old Mother Hubbard
Went to the cupboard,
To give her poor Dog a bone,
When she came there
The cupboard was bare,
And so the poor Dog had none.

JOHN McLOUGHLIN, Publisher, N. Y.

An American version published in the nineteenth century

She went to the seamstress
To buy him some linen;
When she came back
The dog was spinning.

She went to the hosier's
To buy him some hose;
When she came back
He was dressed in his clothes.

The Dame made a curtsy,
The dog made a bow;
The Dame said, Your servant;
The dog said, Bow-wow.

This wonderful dog
Was Dame Hubbard's delight,
He could read, he could dance,
He could sing, he could write;

She gave him rich dainties
Whenever he fed,
And erected this monument
When he was dead.

Anne Perriam, Exmouth's 'Warrior Woman'

By the time that Sarah Catherine Martin was publishing *Old Mother Hubbard* a Devon wife had just finished her naval career. Mrs Anne Perriam was eulogized throughout the country as a 'Warrior Woman' at her death, aged 93, in 1863. In the late 1700s she had

Anne Perriam

accompanied her first husband, Edward Hopping, on board naval ships and her work included being a 'powder monkey': for five years she worked for the navy and her skills as a seamstress were useful when working on flannel cartridge cases alongside the gunners. She had served aboard *HMS Orient* and *HMS Crescent* and was part of Nelson's fleet at the Battle of the Nile. In recognition of her service the government awarded her a (low) pension of ten pounds. Mrs Hopping returned to her native Exmouth after her service, remarried and sold fish in the streets of the town. She died in February 1863 and it was noted in the national press she was 'not surrounded by those comforts which her busy life and strange services should have secured her'.[97]

Elizabeth Ann Holman, a Devon navvy

If Anne Perriam read the local newspapers she would have observed and possibly have been bemused, five years before she died, by the attention paid to a young woman in Exeter for working within a male environment.

'Rather Romantic' was how Elizabeth Ann Holman was described at Exeter in 1858. She had been arrested and was in court on a charge of attempting to obtain money by false pretenses. There was considerable interest in her case and Exeter Guildhall was crowded when, in August of that year, Sergeant Isaac Crone of the 19th Regiment of Foot testified against Holman.

The previous week Sergeant Crone had sworn Thomas Pearce as a recruit. The following day his brother, who had attended the swearing-in ceremony, returned to ask 'do you think if I was to go up to the barracks I could see my brother as I have an experiment on the railway and I want a new pair of strong boots'. However, the Sergeant was informed by his pay sergeant that this brother was actually a woman in male clothes. The 'brother' was then taken into custody.

In a private room the sergeant interrogated Holman who denied

British navvies

being a woman and challenged him 'to inspect for yourself'. The sergeant did indeed physically examine Holman who then admitted to being a woman. In court at the Guildhall a magistrate admonished the sergeant: 'I think *that* was not at all creditable to you'.

Holman testified that she and Pearce had travelled to Exeter together. He had told her 'Lizzie, I shall enlist' to which she responded 'Well, you may enlist but I shall want a pair of boots. You may send what money you can spare to your mother. I can work but all I want from you is a pair of boots'. Holman further testified that she had not felt comfortable 'exposing herself' as a female to the regiment and chose to be discreet. She also claimed that the sergeant had used 'rough and summary means' when examining her. The sergeant protested he was a family man.

Holman was described in court. She was:

> 'a short and very boyish looking girl. Her hair was cut short and parted by the side like that of a boy, and she was altogether so well disguised that it was almost difficult to believe that she belonged to the *softer sex'*. Her hands were said to have been hardened by work.

Her father was a retired pay sergeant in Cornwall. Some ten years before, in about 1848:

> 'at the early age of thirteen she took a fancy to male attire and male pursuits. Doffing her female costume she donned that of a boy-labourer and proceeded to work with a hearty good will, driving horses and carts for farmers or anything laborious that came to hand. She was employed on the Cornwall and Tavistock Railways to drive barrows and fill them with earth and her average earnings were fourteen shillings per week'.

Holman explained that her work colleagues understood she was a woman and called her Lizzie. She had met Pearce five years before, they had cohabited and had two children although one had died. Their surviving child was living with her sister. It transpired that she carried a pipe but it was not confirmed in court that she smoked it.

Holman had given up wearing male clothing only during the birth of their children. She told the court that she would rather be transported abroad than live in England in women's clothing.

The judge felt there was nothing discreditable in Holman's conduct and ordered that she be given half a crown which had been left by the examining surgeon as well as money from the poor box. Well-wishers in the courtroom also gave money and it was reported

Holman left 'smiling pleasantly' and determined to continue along 'the path of rough industry'.[98]

Interestingly, Holman had been arrested in Plymouth three years earlier. The local constabulary were looking out for a man of feminine appearance wanted for robbery in Cornwall. She was seen and claimed her name was Simon Holman but upon discovering the police interest in her she admitted her true identity. In court she divulged she had been employed in Devon and Cornwall as a road and field labourer and had worked as a miner without any suspicions she was a woman. Holman claimed to have been employed to drive a miller's cart and said she could carry a sack of flour on her back. Finally, she testified she wore male clothing because it meant she could earn higher wages than as a woman. The Plymouth magistrates advised her to resume wearing clothing appropriate to her sex.[99]

Yet another female navvy in Devon was revealed the year after Holman's appearance in Exeter's Guildhall. On August 17th 1859 a woman was brought before the Newport magistrates and charged with wearing male clothing. For two years she had worked as a navvy on the Exeter railway line but during the rest of the past ten years she claimed to have worked, in male clothes, as a sailor. The woman was dressed in court in seamen's clothes and was 'in her appearance, gait and gestures appeared to be every inch a sailor and in boldness of conduct presented a striking contrast to the quiet looking seaman, her husband, who stood beside her.'

She explained her work history to the court: for ten years she wore male clothing and 'devoted herself to hard and incessant toil'. She had sailed to Quebec and Bombay among other foreign ports 'never shrinking from her share of duty but loading and unloading the cargoes with the remainder of the crew'. She claimed to have carried, on one occasion, seventy sacks of flour between her ship and the shore. It was said 'while at the winch her courage never flagged and her strength never failed'. Her last voyage had been from Truro to Wales for which she was paid £2 5s per month. Her sex had been discovered although she claimed to have worked incognito.

The Sergeant of the Dock Police had pressed charges because she continued to wear male clothing.

The accused stated she had married four weeks previously and had taken employment because her husband was in poor health. She was working as a steward and cook and left the ship because the captain's wife had complained. She asked the police sergeant:

'Did you ever see men in my company?'
'No.'
'Did you ever hear anything bad in my conduct?'
'No.'

In spite of her vigorous defence, the accused stated she wanted to give up her way of life and was waiting for 'her own clothes' to arrive from Truro. On that understanding she was dismissed and left the court in an omnibus 'in order to prevent being mobbed'.[100]

The Welsh case was reported across the country and was a curiosity. It was not, however, the first of its kind. In 1854 another female navvy made the news: this woman was killed near Bradford where she had been working breaking stones for ballast. It was the same line where her husband, another navvy, had died twenty years before.[101] In 1870 a woman was discovered working as a navvy near Sunderland Bridge. She was reportedly adept at 'nipping', the process of sharpening picks, and the gaffer regretted losing 'the masco-feminine nipper'. She was discharged because railway officials thought the 'not over-sensitive minds' of other navvies might object.[102] There had also been a case in 1855 in Cardiff of drunkenness by a sailor who was a woman. In court she wore a Guernsey shirt, canvas trousers, braces, blue cap and her hands were covered with tar. She was unwilling to dress as a woman and the court gave her some 'wholesome advice'.[103]

The employment of women as navvies contrasts with at least one other part of the country, Brighton, where women worked only as cleaners and waiting room attendants.[104] It may be that Devon, with its use of women as mining labour, was more tolerant. It is more likely that the women who were found in male clothing were particularly strong-minded and resolute individuals.

Mrs Partington of Sidmouth

One mysterious early nineteenth century woman from Sidmouth has become one of that resort's most famous figures who has been cited for nearly two hundred years. Mrs Partington became famous and an international figure through the nineteenth century. She was quoted quite freely as was her counterpart, Mrs Malaprop, another popular figure of fun. For example, she was quoted as saying:

'I am not so young as I was once, and I don't believe I shall ever be, if I live to the age of Samson, which, heaven knows as well as I do, I don't want to, for I wouldn't be a centurion or an octagon and survive my factories and become idiomatic by any means. But then there is no knowing how a thing will turn out until it takes place, and we shall come to an end some day, though we may never live to see it'.[105]

Her fame has resulted in some confusion for there were two Mrs Partingtons in the nineteenth century and both of them achieved great fame. The existence of the two women has muddled the memory of Devon's own Mrs Partington.[106] Some have even thought Mrs Partington of Sidmouth was a mere copy of the other, a woman from New England created by Benjamin Penhallow Shillaber. There was discussion in 1850 as to which figure came first but there is no doubt that Sidmouth's Mrs Partington was the original. Devon can

Mrs Partington in 1869, with Gladstone caricatured

thus safely claim to have the first celebrated Mrs Partington who was very different from the international figure of fun.

Devon's Mrs Partington is thought to have lived in one of the two cottages beneath Clifton Cottage on the west side of Sidmouth. In the other cottage lived a fisherman by the name of Bolt reputedly the last to be 'crowned' as 'King' of the port.[107] Mrs Partington rose to prominence with a speech given in 1831 at Taunton in Somerset by the Reverend Sydney Smith, the celebrated wit, writer and reformer. He said:

'The attempt of the Lords to stop the progress of reform, reminds me very forcibly of the great storm of Sidmouth, and of the conduct of the excellent Mrs Partington on that occasion. In the winter of 1824, there set in a great flood upon that town—the tide rose to an incredible height— the waves rushed in upon the houses, and everything was threatened with destruction. In the midst of this sublime and terrible storm, Dame Partington, who lived upon the beach, was seen at the door of her house with mop and pattens, trundling her mop, squeezing out the sea-water, and vigorously pushing away the Atlantic Ocean. The Atlantic was roused, Mrs Partington's spirit was up; but I need not tell you that the contest was unequal. The Atlantic Ocean beat Mrs Partington. She was excellent at a slop or a puddle, but she should not have meddled with a tempest."[108]

Devon's Mrs Partington was recalled in that discussion of 1850 by one writer who noted:

'The "original Mrs. Partington" was a respectable old lady, living, at Sidmouth in Devonshire; her cottage was on the beach, and during an awful storm (that, I think, of November 1824, when some fifty or sixty ships were wrecked at Plymouth) the sea rose to such a height as every now and then to invade the old lady's place of domicile: in fact, almost every wave dashed in at the door. Mrs. Partington, with such help as she could command, with mops and brooms, as fast as the water entered the house, mopped it out again; until at length the waves had the mastery, and the dame was compelled to retire to an upper story of the house.'[109]

In 1831 the *Taunton Courier* had reported Smith's speech and that he had preceded it making it clear how seriously he regarded giving voting rights to a larger portion of the population:

'Mr Bailiff, I have spoken so often on this subject, that I am sure both you and the gentlemen here present will be obliged to me for saying but little, and that favour I am as willing to confer, as you can be to receive it. I feel most deeply the event which has taken place, because, by putting

Mrs Partington in 1875

the two Houses of Parliament in collision with each other, it will impede the public business, and diminish the public prosperity. I feel it as a churchman, because I cannot but blush to see so many dignitaries of the Church arrayed against the wishes and happiness of the people. I feel it more than all, because I believe it will sow the seeds of deadly hatred between the aristocracy and the great mass of the people. The loss of the bill I do not feel, and for the best of all possible reasons — because I have not the slightest idea that it is lost. I have no more doubt, before the expiration of the winter, that this bill will pass, than I have that the annual tax bills will pass, and greater certainty than this no man can have, for Franklin tells us, there are but two things certain in this world — death and taxes. As for the possibility of the House of Lords preventing ere long a reform of Parliament, I hold it to be the most absurd notion that ever entered into human imagination.'

He concluded that 'gentlemen, be at your ease, be quiet and steady, you will beat Mrs Partington'.[110]

Less than a fortnight later a satirical cartoon was printed depicting the Duke of Wellington as Dame Partington attempting to hold back the ocean of reform.[111] It is possible, but unlikely, that Reverend Smith had intended lampooning Viscount Sidmouth, the former First Minister and Home Secretary, who was vigorously opposed to reform. J. M. W. Turner had satirized Sidmouth's scandalous marriage to a much younger woman by producing a painting of a local rock formation which suggested sexual abandon. Chit Rock stood in the sea near Partington's cottage and had been toppled in the same storm.[112] Dame Partington, however, is more likely to have been a very real character of early nineteenth-century Sidmouth. She began, from Smith's speech, to be used to show futile resistance against a great range of nineteenth-century political issues including the ending of African slavery.[113] Her remarkable example continues to be remembered and cited today including in recent Parliamentary debates.[114]

Louisa, Lady Rolle, of Bicton

When Elihu Burrit visited Devon in 1864 he gave an extraordinary description of the occupant of Bicton, the large country house near Exmouth. If true, Lady Rolle was the most remarkable women ever to have lived in the county. He said:

'This Lady is a remarkable woman, without equal or like in England, in one vigorous, well-developed individuality of will and genius. She is a female rival of Alexander the Great.'

As if this praise was not enough, Burritt continued to write:

'If Virgil had lived in her day, he might have been tempted to substitute *Arbores dominamque cano* ['I sing of trees and the lady'] for his famous introductory line [in the Aeneid], *Anna virumque cano* ['I sing of arms and the man']. The world that the Grecian conqueror subjugated was a small affair in space compared with the two hemispheres which this English lady has taken by the hair of the head and bound to her chair of state. It seems to have been her ambition for nearly half a century to do what was never done before by man or woman, in filling her great park and gardens with a collection of trees and shrubs that should be to them what the British Museum is to the relics of antiquity and the literature of all ages. And whoever has

Lady Louisa

travelled in different countries and climates and visits her
arboretum, will admit that she has realised that ambition
to the full.'[115]

Because of her wealth Lady Louisa, widow of John, Lord Rolle,
of Bicton was one of the leading women in Devon. In 1822 Louisa
Trefusis, daughter of the 17th Lord Clinton, had married Lord Rolle.[116]
He is mostly remembered for having fallen, if not rolled, before
Queen Victoria at her coronation in 1838. He was then 88 years old
and may not have appreciated the puns made at his expense using
his surname. His first wife had died in 1820, two years before his
second marriage to Lady Louisa who was aged 28 and her husband
was 72. In addition to her interest in gardening she gave generously
to the church: Lady Louisa paid in part or full for new or readapting

old churches at Otterton, Bicton, Bath and Exmouth. She also endowed the new Bishop of Truro with ten thousand pounds.

Lady Louisa died, aged 90, in 1885 and was described in one obituary as 'firm and determined in disposition, active in her habits'. Another commentator noted she believed in 'good horseflesh, stout carriage and postilions [the rider of a near horse to a coach]'. Her accustomed mode of transport was seen in the late nineteenth century as being antiquated:

'the sight of Lady Rolle's equipage, never with fewer than with four horses, and with a couple of postillions, rattling along from Bicton into Exeter, a veritable relic of half-a-century ago previous. She was also driven at a steady gallop, and was always very wrathful if the journey was not performed within the hour . . . she insisted on starting to the minute and arriving with equal punctuality.'

If the preceding had been meant as mild criticism, what followed was certainly arched. The journalist also wrote:

'People, subordinates and others who have to be ruled like strong rule. Weak-kneed authority only aggravates and unsettles them. And there is every reason to believe that the strong will and clear brain at Bicton brought content and happiness to those beneath them.'

Moreover, she was compared to a medieval baron who 'saw that his vassals knew their duty and did it . . . wherever he looked, wherever he turned within his own lands, he was master'.[117]

A writer in *The World* was even more indiscreet. He recalled the intense interest in the will of Lord Rolle; he left his wife an annuity of £10,000, their home in London and the use of Bicton while she was alive. The estate passed to her nephew.[118] *The World* recounted that Lady Louisa was greatly disappointed and 'manifested her wrath against her deceased lord by burning his clothes, hunting gear and favourite chair and also his bible and prayer book in Bicton Park, the whole making a bonfire which blazed for some hours'. His decision, according to the journalist, was because of the hot-tempered nature of Lady Louisa. On one occasion she had slapped her husband in the face in the drawing room at Bicton in the company of guests. He reportedly responded 'By God Madam, Damn me to Hell if you shan't repent of this'. It was alleged because of this that Lord Rolle denied his widow the estate.[119] All of this has been forgotten and what most Devonians know of Lady Louisa is the extraordinary Glass House at Bicton. It is the most visible symbol of their marriage: it has been represented for many years as a gift between the couple, a token of their love.[120]

Amelia Griffiths, Queen of Algologists

A very different Victorian life from Lady Louisa was lived by Amelia Griffiths who distinguished herself by her research on seaweed and was described by William Henry Harvey, the author of *Phycologia Britannica*, as having 'the happiest knack of finding the rarest and most beautiful plants in the most perfect state'. He dedicated his book to her as 'a lady whose long-continued researches have, more than those of any other observer in Britain, contributed to the present advanced state of marine botany'. Charles Kingsley spent a summer in Torquay in 1854 and gave extraordinary praise to Mrs Griffiths. He wrote:

> 'Torquay may well claim to be the original home of marine zoology and botany in England, for there worked Montague, Turton and Mrs Griffiths to whose extraordinary

Torquay in 1870

powers of research English marine botany almost owes
its existence and who survived to an age long beyond the
natural term of man to see, in her cheerful and honoured
old age, that knowledge may become popular and general
which she pursued for many a year unassisted and alone'.

She was described as *'facile Regina*, the willingly acknowledged
Queen of Algologists'.[121]

She had begun life as Amelia Rogers in 1768 in Pilton, outside
Barnstaple in north Devon, and at the age of 26 married Reverend
William Griffiths, vicar of St Issey in Cornwall. Six years later she
was widowed when her husband died in mysterious circumstances
and she raised their five children on her own. They moved first to
Ottery St Mary before settling in Torquay in 1829.

Her interest in algae was instigated by the Reverend Goodenough,
later the bishop of Carlisle. Griffiths began collected seaweeds
throughout the South West and had several seaweeds named after
her. She was one of several women who collected seaweed, her

daughter Amelia Elizabeth specialized in mosses and Mary Wyatt, a former family servant, produced volumes of specimens of Devon marine algae as *Algae Danmonienses* from 1833 to 1841. Griffiths was a founding member of the Torquay Natural History Society in 1844. She continued her interests through her life and died at her house in Meadfoot Road a few days short of her ninetieth birthday in 1858. She was buried in Torwood churchyard. One visitor had found her in her senior years a 'very intelligent and spirited old lady with a frank pleasant manner and still full of eagerness about her favourite study'.[122]

Viscountess Beaconsfield: from Mary Evans of Brampford Speke to Mrs Benjamin Disraeli of 10 Downing Street

Benjamin Disraeli had two Devon women who became of great importance to him. One rose from an unlikely background to become his wife and it is apparent that they were devoted to one another. She was not, however, a popular woman or at least was the subject of caustic, sniping remarks. One Victorian commentator wrote, in a column entitled 'Fashionable Gossip' in *The Illustrated Household Journal and Englishwoman's Domestic Magazine*, that:

> 'The life story of the late Viscountess Beaconsfield was, it is said, as strange as that of her husband. It appears she was the daughter of a retired army captain named Evans, and in her youth was employed at a millinery establishment at

Lady Beaconsfield

Exeter, living first in Mint Lane, and for a longer period in the old house, which still stands, next to the Acland Arms, St Sidwell. Having casually made the acquaintance of Mr Lewis, a North Devon gentleman, her attractions fascinated him and she became his wife. He was considerably her senior and before long died. She was then living in London, having inherited her husband's fortune, and the fascinating widow was wooed and won by Benjamin Disraeli'.[123]

Although this note was apparently written with great certainty it may not have been correct in all its details. It can be proved that the Viscountess was born in 1792 and baptized in St Sidwell's church on November 14th as 'Marianne daughter of John and Eleanor Evans'.[124]

Benjamin Disraeli

Her father was in the navy and died young. Her mother's family came from Brampford Speke, only a few miles north of Exeter, and it is with them that it has been suggested that the young widow and her family lived. Her mother called Maryanne 'Little Whizzy' or 'Tiddy'. It appears that at aged fifteen Mary Anne Evans moved with her mother to Gloucester to live with an uncle. Three years later they were in Bristol and in 1815 she married Wyndham Lewis, an industrialist who was fourteen years her senior. After living in

Cardiff the couple moved to London, he became MP for Cardiff and she was widowed in 1838 at the age of 46. Six years previously she had met Disraeli who described her as 'A pretty little woman, a flirt and a rattle'. A year after Lewis' death Disraeli married the wealthy and older widow. She became known as 'Mrs Dizzy'.

Critics mocked her dress sense, her 'low' accent and lack of education. One said she was 'flat, angular, under-bred with a harsh, grating voice'. One Devonian, who met her after she married Disraeli, wrote to his wife that he thought she was:

> 'great fun and we made capital friends in the train, though I could not help pitying her husband for the startling effect her natural speeches must have upon the ears of his great friends. Still, there is something very warm and good in her manner which makes one forgive a few oddities'.[125]

She became known for her off-hand remarks. On one occasion she responded to a comment about a lady's pale complexion by re-marking 'Ah, I wish you could see my Dizzy in his bath! Then you would know what a white skin is.' Amongst her papers was found two lines of text which might indicate how she saw herself.

'A spirit I am,

And I don't give a damn.'[126]

Even so, Disraeli found she was an effective campaigner, an able hostess and more than competent at managing the finances. When he resigned as Prime Minister in 1868 Disraeli asked the queen to create his wife Viscountess Beaconsfield. By that time his wife was ill with cancer and died four years later.[127]

Her life in Devon remains, however, a mystery partly because of her habit of giving fictional accounts of her past. Even so, Sir Stafford Northcote of Pynes, the country house near where her grandparents lived, remembered their driving through Exeter during which she pointed out 'the shop where I was a milliner'.[128] The house where she supposedly lived was in Sidwell Street in Exeter adjoining the

Acland Arms which stood on the corner of York Road. That was not one of Exeter's better neighbourhoods but it is interesting to imagine her having spent her first years there. Queen Victoria allegedly said, after first entertaining her to dinner, 'she is very vulgar, not so much in her appearance as in her ways of speaking'. It may be that she kept a Devon accent through her life.[129] Perhaps one of the comments most apposite, if not appealing, was uttered by her husband. He had just returned home after a great political victory and found his 75 year old wife waiting up for him with a Fortnum & Mason's pie and a bottle of Champagne. He told her 'Why, my dear, you are more like a mistress than a wife'.[130]

Benjamin Disraeli's other Devon woman: Mrs Sarah Brydges Willyams of Torquay

Benjamin Disraeli's second Devon woman was an elderly widow of Torquay who struck up an unlikely friendship with both him and his wife. Disraeli is said to have asked a friend in 1851 'Do you know a mad woman living in Torquay called Mrs Brydges Willyams?' She had been writing letters to him which he had ignored except to ask a Devon friend if indeed a lady resided at the address. But then one letter, which invited him to become her executor and residual legatee, caused him to pause. He was reassured she was sane and eventually accepted her offer. They then embarked on a friendship which comprised a twelve-year correspondence of several hundred letters and annual visits by the Disraeli's to Torquay. The Disraeli's first came in August 1853, when the Russian Royal Family was in the resort, and stayed at Webb's Royal Hotel. They returned to Torquay through to 1862[131] and became part of the social scene in the resort.

They never stayed with Mrs Willyams but while in Torquay were constantly in her company.[132]

At that time Disraeli was a leading national politician, and would soon become Chancellor of the Exchequer, but in 1851 was a complete stranger to Mrs Willyams. She was later described by Sir Philip Rose, Disraeli's political agent, as:

'a lady of advanced age, of moderate fortune, inherited from her own family, but of great intelligence and considerable intellectual powers and had an enthusiastic pride in the race from which she sprung, this in fact was the tie that first attached her to Mr Disraeli, and secured her devoted attachment to him.'[133]

Mrs Willyams' Jewish family had interests in Jamaica which had made them wealthy. Her particular interest in Disraeli arose because they were both Christians with Jewish parentage. Madame Lionel de Rothschild described her in 1862 as:

'The female Croesus, who is likely, or unlikely to leave her wealth to Dizzy. She has piercing black eyes, wears a jet black wig, with an enormous top knot, no crinoline, is quite

A Sketch taken at Torquay Devon in 1853

Mrs Sarah Brydges Willyams as caricatured in 1853

Mrs Willyams
with Mr Disraeli,
1853

a miser, starves herself into a skeleton, except when her
adored Disraeli is here, is ninety-seven years of age, keeps
neither horses, nor carriages, nor men servants—only an
enormous watchdog to protect her and her gold.'

Sir Philip recalled that the two became close friends ('the
acquaintance thus formed grew and ripened into a most intimate
friendship')[134] and Mrs Disraeli appears to have been just as
enthusiastic. Not only did they exchange letters but also gifts
including books, flowers and food. Because he was an important
politician Disraeli was sent upmarket food from various sources
and he forwarded some of this to Torquay; Mrs Willyams had a
blackcock from Drummond Castle, grouse from Lord Willoughby
and venison from the Queen. In return Mrs Willyams dispatched
fish from Brixham including turbot, sole, lobster and prawns.
Disraeli was a witty correspondent. To thank Mrs Willyams for
Devon fish he wrote:

'Yesterday a party of Torquay visitors arrived and were
most hospitably received. There was a great entertainment
given in their honour, at which no less a personage than
our distinguished county member, the Right Hon. B.

Disraeli, was, what the reporters call 'observed' and his Lady . . . Several members of the highly fashionable family of the Mullets were present and we were charmed at the tender grace and fascinating freshness of some of the junior members of the highly popular family of Prawn'.[135]

On one visit Mrs Willyams showed the Disraelis the scenery of Devon. They travelled to Ugbrooke, Berry Pomeroy Castle and the along the river Dart.

Disraeli last wrote to Mrs Willyams on the 5th of November of 1863 and she died six days later in Torquay. Her body was transported to Disraeli's home and buried in the nearby church. The three, Mrs Willyams and the Disraelis were eventually interred together. Her estate was valued at nearly £40,000, which would be the equivalent of several million pounds today, and Disraeli received over £30,000. [136] Some of the property left to him was stolen in a burglary but was later recovered.[137]

Mrs Willyams, a figure not otherwise notable in Torquay, created for herself an unlikely and remarkable friendship with one of Britain's most distinguished politicians. The reasons for it having endured and flourished for more than a decade lie not only with the sharpness of her character but the qualities of her personality.

Mount Braddon, top rigtht, as depicted in the 1830s

Two female pharmacists in
Victorian Paignton

Twenty-five years after the death of Mrs Willyams two women began work as pharmacists in Torquay.[138] Miss Louisa Stammwitz and Miss Annie Neve established a pioneering practice at Paignton. There were then only two other female pharmacists in the country.[139] What is remarkable about these two women was not merely their rarity as women in pharmacy but the difficulties they overcame to become professionally qualified. Louisa Stammwitz had registered as a Pharmaceutical Chemist in 1878 and after nine years working in London she moved to Torbay to open the pharmacy. The Pharmaceutical Society of Great Britain had resisted the admission of women but finally relented in 1879. Neve had qualified in 1884.[140]

In 1892 Stammwitz related her thoughts on her chosen profession. She said:

'pharmacy is undoubtedly a very suitable profession or business, as you will, for women, but so long as "keeping shop" involves loss of social status few will go into business . . . you wonder why women prefer the medical profession to pharmacy. I think this loss of caste is one, if not the chief reason; another is the difficulty of obtaining business training, as chemist have hitherto refused to employ women in their shops or take them as apprentices. At present few pass the pharmaceutical examinations, although many are employed as unqualified dispensers in hospitals. Most people would be surprised to learn how many women do hold dispensaries in hospitals'.[141]

They lived at 2 Palace Avenue in Paignton in 1887 but moved a year later to Ambleside in Cockington.[142] Not long afterwards they moved to Reigate. Why they did not stay in Torbay has not yet been determined. It could have been that the resort was too conservative to accept women as pharmacists. Even so, the two women continued together: Louisa Stammwitz appears to have been living with Annie Neve in Croydon where she died in 1916.[143]

The Misses Skinners and their Hotel of Rest for Women in Business at Babbacombe, 1878 to 1971

In August 1878 two Victorian innovators, Miss Caroline E. Skinner and her sister Miss Emily Skinner, who were then in their mid-fifties, introduced a new concept[144] to Devon: they opened 'The Hotel of Rest for Women In Business' at Babbacombe outside Torquay.[145] The two women were near neighbours, they lived nearby in a house named Bayfield, and according to the census of 1881 were living on their own means. They were originally from Stockton-on-Tees and had been born in Darlington near Durham. The two women were then in their early forties and became internationally known for their long service to women in business. One journalist, many years after they embarked on this course, described them in an article entitled 'Gentlewomen Who Devote Their Lives to the Poor' as 'gentlewoman of independent fortune and high culture'.[146]

The idea came to them whilst they were shopping in Edgware Road in London. They were:

> 'much struck with the tired and wan faces of the assistants who served us from behind the counters. We thought how delightful it would be to get them to Babbacombe for a short holiday and how charmed and refreshed they would be by the pure air and a sight of the blue waters of the beautiful bay'.

They returned to Devon, consulted friends and rented a small cottage which accommodated six guests. It was hoped that a holiday would prevent illness and help improve the lives of women.[147] The two women later stated their aims had been not merely to create a superior boarding house but to put 'beauty, joy, colour, warmth and light' into their guests' lives.[148]

The first arrivals were four young women who worked in Regent Street in London and arrived in an omnibus but only one got off in order to inspect the building. Caroline Skinner later recalled:

Ferny Combe and Ferny Bank

92

The drawing room at Ferny Bank

'She looked rather askance at the cottage and then returned to the other girls and said *you can get out, she is a lady*, referring to myself. On entering one of the rooms the same girl remarked to her companions *they have the best thin china* and going into the pretty bedrooms, and seeing the manner in which they were decorated she observed *I think we will stay*. I replied *My dear girl, did you really think of doing anything else?* And she answered *We thought it was one of those institution places.*'[149]

In 1889 the committee comprised the Misses Skinners and Margaret Roberts, the author of *Mademoiselle Mori, A tale of modern Rome*, who lived nearby in Torquay at Florence Villa.[150] Eight years earlier it numbered among its patrons the Duchess of Sutherland, Countess Spencer, the Countess of Glasgow and the Countess of Sandwich.[151] The original committee included the Duchess of Sutherland who died in 1888.[152] She lived at Sutherland Tower on Warberry Hill and had recently entertained the Princess of Wales in Torquay.[153] The other member was Reverend John Henett, vicar of Babbacombe.[154] Another backer was Sir Walter Besant, the novelist

The Misses
Skinners' in the late
1800s

and crusader for the urban poor. He visited the House of Rest and
became one of the supporters.[155] The important connections that
these people brought no doubt helped the success of the enterprise.

The idea of a holiday place for single women working in trade
proved to be popular. Features about it appeared in a number of
publications including *The Monthly Packet of Evening Readings for
Members of the English Church, Pall Mall Gazette, Women's Penny, The
Sunday Magazine, Murray's Magazine, The Liverpool Mercury.*[156] The
Misses Skinners also wrote pieces themselves. Caroline Skinner,
for instance, penned 'How to make the most of life – an address to
business women in the holiday season' for the *Girl's Own Paper.*[157]
Most of the articles were written by other women. For instance,
Maude Stanley described it in *Clubs for Working Girls* in 1890:
'At Babbacombe in Devonshire the Misses Skinner have built a
delightful home of rest for business girls, who are taken in for five
shillings a week if they have a subscriber's letter, or without for
twelve shillings, and have a return ticket at the price of a single fare.
This is for the higher class of work-girls'.[158] Another story was placed
in the *Girl's Own Paper* which, like all the others, gave considerable
praise to the venture.[159]

94

A heartfelt description came from the pen of Evelyn Whitaker, a novelist, in about 1889. She described it in a letter to a friend. Of shop girls suffering from over-work she wrote:

'Oh! Kate, what would you like to do for them? I know what you will say. Take them quite away, and let them rest, at any rate, for a few weeks; put them in a comfortable arm-chair, in a pretty room with pictures and tasteful things about, with a piano and flowers, and with windows looking on to a garden with soft grass and singing birds, and, perhaps, beyond that the sea, such a sea as one sees in Devonshire, deep, deep blue with great bars of purple cloud-shadows and reflections; and you would like to know there was a little bed, soft and white like yours and mine, ready for those weary, weary limbs and aching heads, in a dainty, lady-like bedroom, where they can have their sleep out. And when they have slept a little of the weariness out of their eyes, and a little of the dull bitterness out of their hearts, you would like to show them all sorts of lovely countrified things, sweet banks, with primroses growing, and young ferns uncurling; thrushes' nests, with warm, blue-speckled eggs; larks singing high in the sunshine; the sun setting in crimson glory over the sea; soft, little waves rippling upon a silver white beach; and the great calm moon drawing her silver pathway across the sea. Think what it would be to take such memories back into the hot work-rooms and close shops, among the walls of boxes and the miles of ribbons! I think it would make life worth living.

And this is just what has been done, what we can help to do. At Babbacombe, near Torquay, a holiday house was opened eight years ago for a house of rest for women in business. It will receive thirty visitors. They are not "patients" or "cases," but visitors, and Ferny Hollow is as nearly as possible a pleasant country house, without any vexatious rules or tiresome interference. It is all pretty and tasteful, such as we have been imagining just now. There is a large drawing room with sofas, arm-chairs, pictures, piano, books, and flowers, and upstairs the pretty bedrooms are not dormitories or wards, but each holds two or three little white beds, round which dainty curtains may be drawn when privacy is desired, and the rooms are called "the rose room," "the green room," "the peacock room," "the violet room," and the walls are tinted to suit their names. And I need not tell you what awaits the girls when, after a good rest, they venture out of Ferny Hollow. You know what South Devon is, and above all Babbacombe; you know the blue sea, and the ruddy cliffs, and the green meadows, and the white marble beach. You know the lovely Devonshire lanes and combes, and the flowers that spring everywhere, and the ferns and moss. How beautiful it is! But what must it be to these girls, many of whom have never had a holiday, never seen the sea, never picked a primrose? "It is like heaven," said one. "It must be easy to be good here," said another. I do not think they debate whether life is worth living at Babbacombe.

I am afraid of making my letter too long, or else I should like to tell you how perfectly happy the girls are there; of the bathing and boating and excursions, of the picnics on the beach and in the woods, of the pleasant evenings of music and games, of the friendships made there, of the stores of health and life they carry away with them; and not only health and life, but hope and courage, and faith in human kindness and in God's great goodness. But if (as I am sure you would) you would like to hear more, send a stamped envelope to Miss Skinner, Bayfield, Babbacombe, and she will tell you all about it much better than is in the power of your affectionate.'

By the time this was written the Rest House had had several incarnations: it was a succession of buildings named Ferny Combe, Ferny Hollow and Ferny Bank. The enterprise outgrew the original

The Skinners' enterprise in the late 1880s

cottage in about 1879 and moved to Delamer in Babbacombe Road where 15 guests could be accommodated. The following year the Misses Skinners took the adjoining property and the numbers of guests went up another 22. It was then called Ferny Hollow but in 1887 they moved again: they bought the freehold of another house on The Downs, which they renamed Ferny Bank.[160] Shortly afterwards another adjoining property was purchased and the total number of possible guests stood at 85. In 1900 they expanded again: a new wing was built which 'might truly be described as a harmonious study in reds'. It housed another 30 guests.[161]

By 1900 the summer household numbered a hundred women comprising the guests, matrons and servants. By that date the guests were shop assistants, milliners, dressmakers, clerks, postal employees, cashiers, teachers, typists and art workers. The Misses Skinners described them as being 'eminently respectable'. Some 500 to 600 women from throughout the country visited each year and generally stayed for a fortnight or three weeks. Many kept returning year after year. The women either paid themselves or were sponsored.

In 1887 Dinah Marie Craik, another novelist, recorded details of some of the women then staying at The House of Rest. One was a mantle-maker who:

> 'lives mostly on bread and tea; barriers bread and butter for her dinner to her place of business as it takes her three hours to walk there and back. A kind forewoman paid for her coming to the House of Rest. She is a pretty, graceful girl of twenty. She said once with a sigh *It is so hard to keep respectable.*'[162]

The women enjoyed a variety of amusements including a tennis court, croquet ground, skittles, bowls, swings, see saws, hammocks and there was boating, swimming and excursions into the countryside. Indoors there was a gymnasium, extensive library, a piano for singing dancing and parlour games. Religious observance was by choice: there were prayers every morning but this was optional and no pressure, according to the Misses Skinners, was placed on agnostics or atheists.

The success of the House of Rest led to imitations in Sweden and Russia. Miss Skinner had been on holiday in Germany and there, by chance, met a woman who had helped start a similar establishment in Sweden.

In 1895 the two Misses Skinners were painted by Ida Verneer, a Royal Academy painter, and the picture was hung in The House of Rest. It has recently been sold. In 1918 Caroline Skinner died, aged 81, as did her sister Emily, aged 86, four years later.[163] The House of Rest however stayed in business: by the start of the Second World it had become the House of Rest and Holiday Home for Business Girls[164] and during the war itself it was occupied by female students of the National Training College of Domestic Subjects.[165] The House of Rest finally closed in 1971, after nearly a hundred years of work. It was still attracting up to 600 women every year but the chairman of the trust commented 'the people it was originally designed to benefit were low-paid shop girls in London. There really is no need for that sort of thing any longer.' Funds were not sufficient to cover the costs and the property was sold.[166]

Two Devonport Dames: Aggie Weston and Sophie Wintz, the Sailors' Friends

Just as the Misses Skinners were actively working in Torquay for the welfare of business women two other local unmarried ladies were similarly involved in looking after sailors in Plymouth. These two women, born in the first decade of the Victorian era, became internationally lauded for their pioneering work and deserve to be regarded as amongst the leading women of Plymouth. Neither were born there but both were buried in the port with full naval honours.

Agnes Elizabeth Weston was born in London in 1840 and had the highest public profile of any woman in Plymouth in the nineteenth century. Sophia Wintz appears to have accomplished as much but was not fully recognized in her lifetime, or since, for her contribution.

Aggie, as she was later known, was the daughter of a wealthy barrister and inherited sufficient wealth which gave her an independence to pursue her own course of life. Her early life was not unduly remarkable. In 1845 the family moved to Bath where she was educated at home and in private schools. One of her main interests was playing the organ but it was her religious and social welfare activities that were to change Devon. She has been remembered as a 'philanthropist and temperance activist' but during her lifetime she was known as 'the sailor's friend' and even as 'the mother of the British navy'.

Religion was central to her life. As an evangelical Anglican she

Dame Aggie Weston

was heavily involved in her early years in religious and social welfare activities: work amongst the young in Sunday school teaching and in visiting the ill in hospital gradually extended to an interest in the provision of recreation rooms and activities in army barracks. Her work for a soldiers' institute laid the path for what became her life work, facilities for naval ratings in this country and abroad.[167]

The temperance cause became paramount. She later recalled, in her autobiography *My Life Among The Bluejackets*, an incident which prompted her to become teetotal. She had spoken at a temperance meeting and several people came up to her to sign the pledge. One was a drunken chimney sweep who had two friends with him.

> '*Our chum is going to sign the pledge* said one of his friends, *he's about sick of the drink, and he's going to give it up, aren't you Jim?* Yaas* answered Jim, *give me the pen.* He stood for a moment

Dame Weston's biography

balancing the pen in his hand and looking me straight in the face and he said in the Somerset dialect *before I zigns, I want to ask this lady one question. Be you a teetotaller, Miss?'*

Weston had to admit she was not and he decided to do what she did: 'take a glass sometimes for the benefit of my health'. She wrote 'That night, I saw my duty very plainly, and I enrolled my name in the pledge book, heartily wishing that I had done so before this poor fellow came forward.'[168]

In 1872 Weston turned her attention from soldiers to sailors. She came to Plymouth, where she had family, and there, for the second time, met Sophia Wintz, seven years her junior. She became her closest colleague and eventual successor. Weston's work lay initially in a correspondence mission and was similar to the earlier work of the Reverend George Charles Smith, founder of the seamen's Bethel movement. She wrote *Monthly Letters* which went to every British naval ship and also a magazine entitled *Ashore and Afloat*. The latter is still produced.

Weston began her missionary work in Plymouth and her first success lay in opening the Wintz family home, namely the kitchen, to sailors. It then progressed to developing institutional facilities with overnight accommodation. They were named the Sailors' Rest and, afterwards, they were designated the Royal Sailors' Rest. Weston was also active in the Royal Naval Temperance Society. Her concern was to give sailors an alternative to public houses and brothels.

Weston became the public face of the movement. She lectured to audiences across the country and raised great sums. Dedicated

The Devonport Sailors' Rest

The Two Dames on a Japanese vessel

buildings were opened in Plymouth in 1876 and Portsmouth in 1881. Miss Weston played a dominant role and this has somewhat obscured the part that others might have played.

One of those figures was Sophia Wintz. The two women had met in Bath at a bible meeting in November 1872 but were not introduced. Weston later recalled her as 'young, fair, golden-haired, the embodiment of health and vigour'. She had 'wondered who she was and I am afraid I thought more of the unknown visitor that morning than of Mr Bassett's prophetical explanations!'[169] A few months later Weston was invited by relations to come to Plymouth where she wanted to do missionary work amongst the sailors. At the same time she received a letter from unknown woman also at Plymouth asking her to lecture to sailor's wives and offering accommodation in her mother's house. Weston agreed to speak and travelled to Plymouth where she:

'was shown into the drawing room and in a moment a young woman arrived. I was amazed; I had pictured an elderly and rather severe person and here was the very reverse, all youth, brightness and smiles and to crown it all, this was the very same lady that I had met at the class at Bath . . . we became friends at once, and have continued friends ever since, although forty-two years have passed over our heads. There is a very grave suspicion among members of the opposite sex that women cannot remain friends for any length of time – they are sure to quarrel and part'.[170]

Two of Wintz's near relations were Admirals. Her mother lived at Penlee Villas in Stoke Dameral in Plymouth and this was initially their base. In 1901, nearly thirty years after they first met, the two women moved into a house at Hindhead in Surrey. There 'we felt

The Surrey home of the two ladies

that we might be able to accomplish a home and do our work as well'.[171] Seventeen years later Weston was awarded the Dame Grand Cross and died that year, on 23 October 1918, in her Sailor's Rest in Devonport. The obituaries praised her lifelong service.

Her funeral took place in the dockyard's church and she was the first woman to be given full naval honours. The King was represented by Vice-Admiral Thursby and in addition to 2,000 British sailors there were representatives of the Royal Marines, the Army, the Royal Air Force, the W.R.N.S and the American Navy. Lines of armed 'Blue Jackets' were drawn up along the road from the Royal Sailor's Rest to the church and the coffin was placed on a gun carriage, covered with the Union Jack and drawn by sailors. Two admirals followed on foot. The coffin was interred in Devonport at the Weston Mill cemetery.[172] Her memorial stone proclaims her 'The Sailor's Friend'.

At the time of Dame Weston's death Admiral Beresford wrote to *The Times* in praise of her work and concluded 'her lifelong friend and helper Miss Wintz . . . will receive the sympathy of the navy

Dame Weston's memorial in 1919

Dame Aggie Weston

in her loss'.[173] Miss Wintz continued as superintendent of the homes until she died eleven years later on 16 January 1929. She was appointed Dame Commander of the Order of the British Empire and was also given a full naval funeral in the same church. She was buried in Dame Weston's grave. In 1917 Dame Weston wrote of her friend Sophia:

> 'the history of our interwoven lives appears in this book, and if it is read bearing in mind that in all that I have done she has borne at least half the burden, and should have half the honour, something of her life work will be understood . . . Of all the noble and disinterested friendships hers will easily rank first, with marvelous talent for organization and management, she has kept this great work going, and has steadily obscured herself to give me the first place. Hers' has been a grand life indeed.'[174]

The importance of the contribution of the two women is certain while the exact nature of their personal relationship remains elusive.

Women's emancipation and the struggle for rights

Just as the Misses Skinners and the two Plymouth Dames were involved in their good works there were many dozens of other Devon women caught up in the national struggle to give women equal rights as men.

The struggle for women to gain the right to vote began in the middle of the nineteenth century and continued for several generations. Some argued for parity with men: Parliamentary legislation in 1832, 1867 and 1884 expanded the number of men eligible to vote and increasingly women argued for the same rights. Other women wanted all women to be able to vote, not just those with high levels of wealth. In 1869 women were granted the right to vote in local elections if they were the heads of the household and unmarried. Twenty-five years later, in 1894, this was extended to similar women who were married. In 1918 some women over the age of thirty were given the right to vote in national elections (as well as men over 21) and it took another eleven years before that right was extended to all women.

Devon played a part in these campaigns. Like many parts of the country it effectively began in the 1860s and local women worked for more than sixty years to help achieve it. This was similar to the county's campaign against African slavery that began in the 1770s and did not end until the late 1830s.

After a generation of campaigning the first decade of the twentieth century saw increased activity. The county had the two groups of women campaigners who were active throughout the country. The first was the National Union of Women's Suffrage Societies, the body established in the nineteenth century which tried to work with the political system for change. The second group was a newer organisation which quickly became known as 'militant':[175] Mrs Emmeline Pankhurst and her daughters were the leading figures of the Women's Social and Political Union and argued that direct action was needed. Members of this group became known as Suffragettes. These groups occasionally worked together but were also rivals.

Much of the activity was in holding meetings and trying to gain support amongst the population, both male and female. There were also events such as that of 1911 when Dr Mabel Ramsay held a census resistance party at her house in Plymouth. Their point was to peacefully disrupt the machinery of the state.[176] Twenty women slept on couches, chairs and rugs but left before five in the morning and refused to fill in details of the census form. She later noted:

'I well remember the oldest one present. She was rather feeble physically but her powers of resistance were strong and not confined to the census, for my repeated efforts failed to induce her to accept a bed. She was determined to "suffer for the cause" and sat in a chair the whole night through. Of course, her refusal of preferential treatment and subsequent sacrifice of personal comfort were pointless in the circumstances, but the episode illustrates, rather touchingly I think, the ardent spirit prevalent then amongst those women who were dominated by the urge to redress great injustice. I remember I spent the night on my consulting room couch – a hard bed!'[177]

She added 'I can only say that every bed in the house was occupied and a good deal of floor space. No prosecutions took place resisting the census officer for it was found there were too many Suffragists to prosecute them all!'[178] She had left her mother to face the census collector who left the house 'somewhat baffled'.[179]

In April 1913 Winston Churchill visited Plymouth as First Lord of the Admiralty and Smeaton's Tower on the Hoe was daubed with white paint in his honour. On the Sound side unknown activists wrote 'To Churchill, No security till you give the women votes, no matter how big the navy' and on the city side was written 'To save the State from shipwreck give women the vote'. One shelter had a message 'To Churchill, no rest for the government while they torture us women' and another had simply 'Votes for Women'. Even more serious was the cutting of telephone wires at Lipson. Both events were attributed to Suffragettes.[180]

The outbreak of the First World War brought a cessation in the suffrage campaign and their support for war work. Mrs Emmeline Pankhurst came to Plymouth that year, in November, and told an audience 'If you go to this war and give your life, you could not end your life in a better way, for to give one's life for one's country for a great cause is a splendid thing'[181]

The struggle in Devon had some key local moments. These in-cluded the campaign at Newton Abbot in the election of 1907 to

109

1908, the pursuit of Prime Minister Asquith to Clovelly Court in 1909, the hunger strikes of three Suffragettes in 1909 and again of Mrs Pankhurst in 1913, and the Pilgrimage in 1913 from Land's End to London.

The Election at Newton Abbot, 1907 to 1908

The Parliamentary Election at Newton Abbot in December 1907 and January 1908 was the most violent of all the local campaigns that involved Devon women. On the 16th of December the first appearance was made by the Suffragettes and they continued until the election results were announced at which point an angry mob brutally assaulted the women. Mrs Pankhurst spent Christmas that year at Teignmouth with Mrs Mary Gawthorpe, an organizer for the WSPU in Lancashire.[182]

Both national groups of campaigners were active in the constituency. Mrs Emmeline Pankhurst spent considerable time in the area[183] and backed the Unionist candidate whereas the NUWSS decided neither candidate was sufficiently committed to giving women the right to vote. Open air meetings were held but at one in the Market Square Mrs Pankhurst found the crowd too raucous for her to be heard.

It was assumed the Liberal candidate would win and the local party printed a mourning card mocking the efforts of the Suffragettes.

'In memory of the Suffragettes and
Tariff Reformers who fell asleep
At Mid-Devon on January 7, 1908'[184]

Mrs Pankhurst and supporters in Newton Abbot

Thus there was pandemonium in Newton Abbot when Mrs Pankhurst's candidate won. The opponent's supporters pelted her and Mrs Nellie Martell, another Suffragette who had campaigning experience in Australia, with clay, rotten eggs and snowballs studded with stones. Mrs Pankhurst later recalled:

'suddenly we were confronted by a crowd of young men and boys, clay-cutters from the pits on the edge of town. These young men, who wore the red rosettes of the Liberal Party, had just heard of their candidate's defeat. One of them pointed to us, crying *They did it!*'

The two women ran into a grocery shop and were hounded out through the back door, pushed to the ground and kicked. Both were covered in mud and Mrs Pankhurst suffered an injured ankle. She had regained consciousness to find herself surrounded by a ring of silent men 'in their drab clothes smeared with yellow pit-clay

Suffragetttes Campaigning in Newton Abbot

and they seemed so underfed, so puny and sodden that a poignant pity for them swept over me. Poor souls I thought and then I said suddenly *Are none of you men*?' The two women were then rescued by the police who waited two hours until it was safe to take them to Teignmouth.[185]

The mob might have intended to put her in a barrel and another account claimed they wanted to throw her into the river.[186] A few days afterwards Mrs Pankhurst wrote to *The Times* they had had great influence in defeating the government's candidate and that the political parties were realizing the importance of women in elections.[187]

The Prime Minister at Clovelly Court in 1909

In the 1870s meeting began to be held in North Devon but as late as 1911 a visiting NUWSS speaker claimed 'the district was quite new ground when I came here some weeks ago'. Shortly afterwards Suffragettes were accused of setting fire to two North Devon buildings. One of them was Hollerday House in Lynton. It was cited as an arson attack by suffragettes and national and local papers reported loud explosions were heard.[188] There was just as little evidence to link them to the fire at Bideford Pavillion the following year. It was suggested the Suffragettes could be responsible given the proximity of the Westward Ho! Golf Club which was one of the first in the country to admit women: there were 'persistent rumours' of militant suffragettes playing golf there.[189]

Earlier still, in 1909, there was a curious Suffragette event in North Devon. Over Whitsun Prime Minister Herbert Asquith held a house party for colleagues at Clovelly Court, then the home of the Honorable Arthur Asquith. According to one Suffragette he received a note from his wife during Sunday service that three suffragettes were in the building: Elsie Howey, Jessie Kenney and Vera Wentworth had also travelled to Clovelly. Jessie Kenney later recalled 'Poor old Asquith, we really got on his nerves which was what we wanted to do. One Whitsuntide, three of us turned up at Clovelly where he was spending his holiday, and on the Sunday we went to church. We were all dressed up – one in purple, one in white and one in green. And we sat there very quietly as demurely as we could. Asquith came in and took his seat with his wife who hated us like poison. She nudged him and passed him a note. He looked up and saw us. He passed a note to someone else as much as to say, "Protect me as best you can". Afterwards he left the church by a side door.' [190] A report in a local newspaper provides more details:

'Immediately after the service he was followed by two or three Suffragettes who pressed their familiar questions. Mr Asquith endeavoured to ignore their importunities by addressing himself to Lady Bentinck with whom he was walking. The walk from the Church to the Court grounds is short so that the Suffragettes did not have much chance of annoying the Premier, who was, however, followed to the door.'

The three women were not finished with hime. The following day they:

'renewed their attentions, managing to elude the police watchers and to reach the private golf course at Clovelly Court by scaling cliffs. While one of them occupied the attention of a policeman in parleying, sometime later, the two others rushed towards Mr Asquith who was playing golf. They seized him by the arm, but had only time for a word or two before the police came up. The Prime Minister said to the constables *take these women away, I refuse to speak to them* and the Suffragette emissaries, whose names and addresses were taken by the police, were escorted off the grounds.'

Kenney recalled that night the women departed and were watched with great interest by the locals who did not realize that shortly afterwards, at Bideford, the three of them deposited their luggage and walked the ten miles to Clovelly. They went to the country house at two in the morning and decorated the rhododendrons with 'Votes for Women' mottoes. The local journalist noted the women's ingenuity and imagination. He recorded banners were placed in the centre of the lawn and the garden was decorated with placards, pamphlets and broad sheets. The women then walked back to Bideford and caught an early morning train to London.[191]

The arrest of three Suffragettes at Exeter in 1909

In 1909 three 'young militant Suffragettes' were arrested and incarcerated at Exeter Prison for disturbing a public meeting with Earl Carrington on July 31st at Victoria Hall in Exeter. Two of the unmarried women, Elsie Howey and Vera Wentworth, were reportedly well-known in Torbay where they had been campaigning and had recently been agitating in Clovelly. *The Times* reported they lived in Clement's Inn in London then the party's headquarters. A few months earlier both women had interrupted a similar meeting in Bristol. Elsie Howey was an unpaid organizer for the WSPU in Devon and particularly active in Torquay. She was known partly for her dressing up as Joan of Arc on horseback. Vera Wentworth succeeded Howey as Plymouth organizer of the WSPU. She was later forcibly fed in gaol in Bristol.[192] In Exeter Prison the women objected to not having First Division status which recognized them as political prisoners. The two later recalled:

'the first thing we did on arriving at the prison was to stand against the wall and link arms, and ask to see the governor who had already appeared on the scene. We explained that, having been placed in the third division, we should feel it our duty to disobey the prison regulations and refuse food until placed in the first division. We also explained that our quarrel was only with the government and not with the prison officials. Everyone seemed to understand this, and we were throughout treated with the utmost consideration compatible with the carrying out of their duty. We refused to go to our cells but were forcibly removed there. We then sang our war songs. Presently we were told to put on prison dress. We refused and were dressed by the wardress and removed to fresh cells, each being placed on a different floor. We were able, however, as the prison is very small, to make each other hear cheers and songs. On Sunday we broke the glass in the spy-holes of our cells so as to be able to converse. We were then removed to basement cells which adjoined each other and were fairly light and airy. Here we again broke our spy-holes and some panes in our windows. We had meanwhile written to the Home Secretary demanding to be placed in the first division.

On Monday morning we were taken before the governor and magistrate and sentenced. Miss Phillips to three, and Miss Wentworth and Miss Howey to two days' close confinement. We immediately broke two more panes as protest, for which we received another day's confinement thus making our sentences equal. We also sang our war songs with more than usual vigour, for the edification of the magistrate. Later in the day the governor came, saying he had a telegram 'from London' with orders to place us in the second division. We replied, of course, that this was not satisfactory and we should continue our protest. Next day we were visited in turn by doctor, chaplain and governor, who all tried to persuade us to take food, the doctor threatening to feed us, if necessary. And when we told him this was illegal he replied he would even certify us insane in order to do so! We laughed at him, of course, and took no notice of his threats. Everyone in the prison was greatly surprised at the way we kept up our strength and spirits. We managed to sing and converse up to the morning of our release though almost too weak to stand'.[193]

The Times reported the two women and Miss Mary Phillips of Bristol were charged with obstructing the police. Each woman refused a fine in favour of imprisonment. Two men were also charged. The women had objected to the meeting being closed to women.[194] Miss Phillips was active in Devon and Cornwall for the WSPU until late in 1909. She had previously lived in Cornwall and in 1913 moved to Plymouth.[195] Local newspapers reported they were on a hunger strike and that Miss Phillips was released early because of her weakened state.

When they were sentenced the court heard the women had attempted to speak to Earl Carrington at the Rougemont Hotel but he eluded them by using a side door. Their subsequent actions outside the hall gave the evening the 'character of a riot' as the women called upon a watching crowd to rush through the police cordon into the entrance. One of the women had supposedly said 'one more glorious rush and rush us inside, don't mind the police.' The women were brought the short distance to the police station but the accompanying crowd tried to rescue them. Two men, one a meter tester from Exe Island and the other a labourer of Belgrave Road, were also arrested for obstruction.[196]

The Pilgrimage to London in 1913

In 1913 Devon women joined a Pilgrimage to London for women's rights. Others from across the country marched for six weeks along eight routes and arrived together at Hyde Park on July 26th. The 'Suffragist Pilgrims' from the South West left Land's End on June 19th and arrived in Plymouth ten days later. They were at Torpoint, wearing green, white and red sashes, and were met by a group of supporters from Devonport. They had with them a caravan and the spectacle attracted a rowdy juvenile crowd. A local journalist reported:

> 'Young gentlemen of ten wished the ladies *three years in prison* and young ladies of about the same age confided that *Mrs Pankhurst won't never get her vote*. There is no doubt a strong juvenile opinion against the enfranchisement of women, and affixed conviction in the same quarters that Mrs Pankhurst is one of the party. Miss Fraser was hailed as that lady, and solemnly told that she ought to be ashamed of herself. These things did not disturb the self-possessed young ladies who were in charge of the van.'

The crowd in Torpoint had been largely sympathetic and the women crossed the ferry to Devonport. The first words they heard in Devon were:

> '*Suffragettes, Bill, Oh, Lord*! so the ladies were greeted when they arrived on the Devonport side, where some dockyardmen were waiting to board the ferry. One of them was spoiling for a war of words. *You can't fight for your country*, he pointed out. *We can go on the battlefield and patch up men who do* was the immediate reply from one of the party. *Got you there, o' man* chimed in another workman and there was some applause. But the controversialist would not go under without an effort. *You go there to get husbands* he returned. This inspiration was received with rather unsympathetic laughter and the warning bell called him to the ferry'.

The women then had a police escort through Plymouth and stopped at Dr Mabel Ramsay's home on North Hill for lunch.[197] They held an open-air meeting in Victoria Park and an evening meeting at the Corn Exchange. About twenty-five women then joined the march to London and they were escorted to the city's boundary by the local constabulary. Another meeting was held at Plympton. Rotten eggs and tomatoes were thrown at various points. Dr Ramsay's mother, then fifty-five years old and described as 'the old lady from Land's End', completed the march and delivered the message at Hyde Park: 'the women of the West demand votes for women'.[198] Two of them were later recalled by Dr Ramsay:

'Mrs [Annie] McMillan and her sister Miss Symons were in the Land's End group. The former is one of the smallest women I ever knew but she has the spirit of a giant, and when she decides that a certain way to take is the right way she carries on. At one time she was an actress and played in *Charley's Aunt*, when it was first put on the stage. Many people will remember that after the 1939 to 1945 war she played a part in the Plymouth film *The Way We Live*.'[199]

The march through Devon took place from June 29th and by July 5th a group was leaving Exmouth for Exeter: there was an open air meeting in that resort the night before. Women from surrounding towns and villages, including Sidmouth, Budleigh Salterton, Topsham and Torquay, then converged at Exeter: they processed through South Street and Fore Street to Gervase Avenue.[200] The march then went to Taunton and eventually London.

Mrs Pankhurst's Hunger Strike at Exeter Prison in 1913

On Thursday, December 4th 1913 Mrs Emmeline Pankhurst was arrested at Plymouth when she arrived on the White Star liner S.S. *Majestic*. She was returning from her third visit to the United States where she had an extensive, and lucrative, lecture tour. She had made a sizeable sum to give to the suffragette cause and had extensive publicity across the United States. The following weekend was the most sensational episode in Devon's suffrage history.

It had been anticipated Mrs Pankhurst would be arrested when she landed in England. She had an outstanding prison sentence through the enacting of the 'Cat and Mouse Act', the common name for the Prisoners, Temporary Discharge for Health Act of 1913. The government had become embarrassed by the Suffragettes' hunger strikes and had initially force-fed the women but this proved controversial. Its response was legislation which allowed prisoners to be discharged on health grounds under a license. The benefit was that the women would begin to eat outside prison and once recovered could be instantly arrested if they broke the law or agitated.

Plymouth's Chief Constable had a reputation for being compliant with the press but on this instance, in the days before Mrs Pankhurst's arrival, he refused to cooperate with them despite their issuing 'dire threats of journalistic vengeance'. The newspapermen had assumed were refused access to Mrs Pankhurst's arrest and had to wait onshore in a scrum. Moreover, after the liner arrived two boats were sent to the ship, neither of which were admitted to being

Mrs Pankhurst being arrested in London

the transport for Mrs Pankhurst, and naval ships were deployed to screen the view from the shore.

It transpired later that the police secretly took Mrs Pankhurst to Saltash and then by stages across Dartmoor to Exeter Prison. Neither the press nor the group of female supporters, termed by one journalist as 'hench-women' and some of whom had arrived from London, were told where Mrs Pankhurst would be landed.[201] They had attracted a large crowd, of several thousand people, at the Great Western Docks.[202] Mrs Pankhurst had been forewarned by a telegram that she would be arrested and shortly before it happened two women, in a fisherman's dory, managed to dash in front of the arresting steamer and called out to her 'The Cats are here Mrs Pankhurst! They're close on you'.[203]

The day after Mrs Pankhurst's secret journey to Exeter there was an announcement that she was there in prison and it was admitted she was on hunger strike. Her supporters travelled from Plymouth

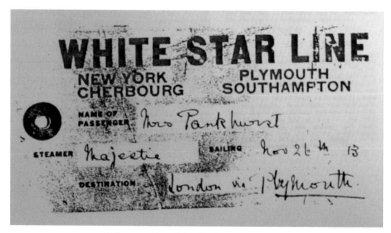

Ephemera from Mrs Pankhurst's voyage

and London, including her daughter Sylvia, and established a picket outside the prison. They also had two motor cars in case Mrs Pankhurst was taken from Exeter. The presence of dozens of picketing Suffragettes attracted young men who 'indulged in rough horseplay' and on two occasions they rushed the women. One Suffragette was in danger of being thrown off the railway bridge and was taken into custody by the police for resisting.[204] By coincidence Millicent Fawcett was lecturing in Exeter. There was 'slight applause' from the audience when she referred to Mrs Pankhurst being in prison in Exeter and although she said she deplored the arrest Fawcett used the occasion to reaffirm their abhorrence of the use of violence.[205]

Mrs Pankhurst was released, after 79 hours in Exeter Prison, at ten pm on the Sunday night and brought by cab to the Great Western Hotel. She was then put in bed and the next morning she, along with her supporters, took a morning train to London.[206] Mrs Pankhurst was told to return a week later. When her supporters heard of the release there was cheering amongst the 5,000 crowd attending a London meeting. Mrs Pankhurst did not return to Exeter but instead travelled to Paris.[207]

It was claimed shortly afterwards that a fire in a Devonport timber yard was retaliation for the arrest. A copy of *The Suffragette* was found at the scene as well as two postcards. On one was written 'our reply to the torture of Mrs Pankhurst and her cowardly arrest here'. On the other was written 'to the government, how dare you arrest Mrs Pankhurst and allow Sir Edward Carson and Mr Bonar Law to go free?' The other side of the card had the words 'votes for women. An answer to the cowardly arrest of Mrs Pankhurst here'.[208]

When Mrs Pankhurst returned to Plymouth a year later she was involved in a different campaign altogether: she was soliciting support for the war. She told her audience that in Plymouth a year previously she was 'a militant Suffragette, I was a convict as I still am. Life is a queer, topsy-turvy thing, isn't it? Here you have a convict whose license has expired and not amnestified, actually asking people to enlist and fight for the country . . . if you go to this war and give your life, you could not end your life in a better way – for to give one's life for one's country, for a great cause, is a splendid thing'.[209]

Dr Mabel Ramsay, Medical Doctor, Suffragette and Soroptomist

One of Plymouth's most notable women in the early twentieth century was Dr Mabel Lieda Ramsay. In addition to her medical career she was committed to the suffragist campaign and was active in promoting women's interests in the decades that followed the First World War. She died in 1954, aged 75, while attending a medical women's conference.[210] More is known of Dr Ramsay than many other local women because she wrote her memoirs 'A Doctor's Zig-Zag Road'.[211]

Dr Ramsay was not Plymouth-born. She began life in London

Dr Mabel Ramsey

in about 1879, the second child of a Naval officer, and spent her childhood partly abroad and in Devon. When she was eight years old the family left Malta. Initially they lived in Tavistock where she had arrived suffering from Whooping Cough. Her cure was to stand each day in the fumes of the local gas works. A fishwife heard the young girl coughing and advised Mrs Ramsay 'if you go to the fish market and buy a live plaice and lie it on the child's chest and leave it to rot, by the time it is rotted the cough will be cured'. Fortunately for the eight year old Mabel her mother resisted the advice. Shortly afterwards the family moved to Plymouth. At 17 Mabel trained as a gymnast in Exeter and later went to high school. The majority of her medical education began in 1900 in Scotland[212] and her specialty was obstetrics and gynaecology.[213]

Dr Ramsay began practicing medicine in Plymouth in 1908 but she found the local medical establishment did not encourage her. She had three failed applications for the post of Medical Officer of the Plymouth Public Dispensary and received a letter from a medical member of the committee informing her that they had passed a resolution that 'no woman doctor would ever be considered as eligible for appointment on the medical staff'. Dr Ramsay discovered, after asking to see a copy of it, that no such resolution had been made. She did not, however, make another application. She had the satisfaction, several years later, when, during the First World War, that they asked her to join them in the Charity and Provident Committee. She served on their medical staff, was Honorary Surgeon-Gynaecologist for eighteen years and placed on the committee. By the time the National Health Service took over the establishment she had also been Honorary Treasurer and Honorary Secretary.

Her medical career also involved service in France during the First World War. She helped establish a Women's Imperial Hospital Unit in a sixteenth-century chateau in Cherbourg in 1914. Conditions were not easy: the sanitation was via buckets to trenches some distance from the building. She served as a Red Cross surgeon at the hospital as well as at another in Antwerp. Dr Ramsay endured the shelling of the hospital and the experience gave her nightmares for many years afterwards.[214]

After the war she became Honorary Secretary, and later President, of the Medical Women's Federation and in 1929 drew attention to the discrepancies between wages given to medical men and women employed by the post office. It was, she wrote, beyond 'the bounds of belief'.[215] Her Plymouth career included being surgeon at the Salisbury Road Hospital and the City Hospital. She was also President of the Plymouth Medical Society.[216]

Ramsay's involvement in women's suffrage began in 1908. She later wrote:

'a few weeks after I had started practice a Miss Robertson, organizer for the National Union of Women's Suffrage Societies (President Mrs Henry Fawcett) called on me and begged me to help form a Plymouth Branch. Curiously enough, just after graduating in 1906, a small book had been given to me entitled *The Subjection of Women* by John Stuart Mill. I had not read it. I proceeded to do so forthwith and, after careful consideration, decided to help to form the

Plymouth branch of the NUWSS of which I subsequently became the Honorary Secretary'.

She became one of the key women in Plymouth involved in the suffrage movement. Ramsay recalled:

'I well remember the day when I had nervously made my first suffrage speech at a public meeting and when a look from my mother, who was sitting in the front room, saved me from bursting out crying. The ice was broken and from that day onwards I went to my places in Devon and Cornwall and Somerset to plead for *Votes for Women*. Thus began my education as a public speaker. Of course, we faced much verbal opposition but, unlike my mother, I never had anything thrown at me.'

In 1930 Dr Mabel Ramsay pioneered the formation of the Plymouth Soroptomist Club.[217] The organisation had recently arrived in Britain from the United States and there were thirty-four members including Nancy Astor. The meeting place was destroyed in bombing in the early 1940s. Among its activities was canvassing for women in the local constabulary.[218]

She has not been entirely forgotten in Plymouth. In 1997 one of Plymouth successor women members of parliament recalled Ramsay in her maiden speech in Parliament as one of the city's most distinguished women.[219] She deserves a distinguished place in the history of Plymouth.

Elsie May Fraser, A Devonport V. A. D. nurse

While Dr Ramsay was working in France operating on Allied soldiers Miss Elsie Fraser was in Plymouth helping them to recover. She may have been a remarkable woman but it is difficult to see how very different she was from one of the many others who acted as V.A.D. nurses in the First World War. The Voluntary Aid Detachment had been set up in 1909 and the majority of them were women. Fraser worked at Ford House Military Hospital in Devonport. Like other nurses, she collected the signatures and artwork of her patients. Her autograph book has survived, a testament to the service she put in to care for soldiers brought home from the battlefields of Europe. Through them we have a sense of the men who wrote them and of the woman they were dedicated to.[220]

Private G. Bryant of the West Yorkshire Regiment was one of the men she cared for. He wrote:

'Far far from Ypres I want to be,
Where German snipers can't shoot at me,
Damp is my dugout,
Cold are my feet,
With nothing but bully and biscuits to eat.'

Perhaps one of the strongest sentiments to come from the scrapbook is the escape she gave the men from their wounds and memories of war on the continent. It may not seem remarkable to posterity, but it might have been so for the men themselves.

The staff and patients at Ford Hospital

Private Vean wrote

'We lay amongst the Dead,
We lay amongst the Ruins,
And when the war is over,
We'll be amongst the doings'

Many of the messages were romantic or mildly suggestive, such as that by Private H. Watters:

'Forget me not my darling,
Although we are apart,
Others may have my company,
But you still have my heart'

Presumably Nurse
Fraser

There was a similar one by 'J. H.':

'When Elsie May remains at home,
She's always good and quiet,
But in the street the other night,
She nearly caused a riot,
She got engaged to fifteen men,
And quiet enjoyed the night,
When someone let her secret out,
And they began to fight.'

Nurse Fraser?

Private C. H. Paton wrote a more poignant verse:

'They can mend a broken aeroplane,
Or a damaged motor car,
They can heal up wounds in a wonderful way,
And never leave a scar.
They can mend our faces, heads & limbs,
However the pain may smart,
But they haven't found the wrinkle yet,
To mend a broken heart.'

Exeter's first female strikers

In the closing months of the First World War a small group of women went on strike in Exeter demanding an increase in their wages: they were being paid five pennies an hour and wanted an extra penny. The women claimed they did not have a living wage. Their strike resulted in 'novel and mildly exciting scenes' in and around the City Collar Works in Old Vicarage Road in St Thomas.

These were not women who had been drafted into factory work because of a shortage of men caused by the First World War; they had been employed there before 1914. Many of them were teenage girls and they marched through the streets carrying banners which read 'Food goes up, why not wages?' and 'Shirkers, why not come out and join us?'. Inflation had been high during the war and had more or less doubled. The strikers were anxious about women from another union who had not joined their strike as well as nine other non-union women. The police kept the two groups of women separate as the workers arrived and left the factory at lunch and evening. After several days of picketing most non-union women had joined them.

Mr Rice, the owner of the factory, claimed that it was unfair for him to pay higher wages when other factory workers were still paying only five pennies an hour. Moreover he suggested that the government had agreed not to increase wages. The strike continued because, as the women insisted, 'the money we get isn't enough to live on and that's the whole point'. It transpired that a government agreement did not involve this strike but Mr Rice continued to refuse to pay the extra penny an hour. After a fortnight his factory closed down and negotiations between the Union and him failed. By the end of the month there was a more important strike: railway workers across the country, including Exeter, stopped working and those events overtook the reporting of the women's strike in St Thomas.[221]

Lady Nancy Astor

Nancy Astor must rank as one of Devon's most famous women. Her becoming the first women to take her seat in the House of Commons has distinguished her and is the main reason for her fame which has somewhat overshadowed the key role she played in Plymouth during the second world war. One biographer termed her a 'society hostess and politician' which description aptly combines her wealth and politics.

Nancy Langhorne was born in 1879, the daughter of a wealthy Southern American who had fought for the Confederacy in the Civil War. It has been suggested that her southern protestant upbringing and personal insecurities 'made her appear puritanical and censorious; in particular she had a lifelong aversion for alcoholic drink and a rooted fear of physical relationships. She told her own children they had been *conceived without pleasure and born without pain*. Later in life she managed to resolve the problem by engaging in a number of safe, platonic affairs.'

At the age of eighteen she married but the union failed and they divorced six years later. She had apparently been 'revolted' by his drinking and sexual demands. The following year she travelled to

Nancy Astor

England and three years later, in 1906, she married Waldorf Astor, later second Viscount Astor. With him she had five children and she is reputed to have once said *'I suppose you all think you're misunderstood* and one replied *We've given up hoping for that . . . All we want is a bit of civility'.*

In 1914 she converted to Christian Science and her religious convictions, along with an adherence to temperance, formed a major part her public personality. She was even said to have tried to convert Joseph Stalin. In 1910 her husband was elected as one of Plymouth's two MPs and when he succeeded to his father's title in 1919 she stood in his place. She received 51 per cent of the vote.[222] A year after Dame Aggie Weston's death, who was the most well-known advocate of temperance in Plymouth, Nancy Astor replaced her.

Neither she nor her husband had a background in supporting women's suffrage. It was only a few years previously that Waldorf Astor publicly declared women should have the vote.[223] Dr Mabel Ramsay recalled later that Astor had promised to support women's suffrage ahead of a public meeting. She wrote

> 'when the day came my telephone was repeatedly rung by some of his supporters, tearfully begging me to prevent him from speaking at the meeting, but he kept his promise.'[224] Had he not changed his mind it would have been difficult for his own wife to have stood for Parliament. Her subsequent career in the Parliament has been described as having passed its peak by the end of the 1920s with fellow MPS finding her 'rather tedious, too lightweight and indiscreet'. In the 1930s she found herself becoming notorious when she was criticized as being a dupe for Hitler. She and her husband were sympathetic to Germany for its treatment after the First World War and this was widely presented in the media as indicative of their politics. Parliamentary colleagues called her 'the Honorable Member for Berlin'.[225] It is interesting that Lady Astor refused to criticize the violence in Plymouth in the mid 1930s when Sir Oswald Mosley's Blackshirts were fighting in the streets. Although her media scrapbook is full of newspaper cuttings about the violence she did not feel the need to comment. This may have been due to her long-standing friendship with Mosley which originated from her first campaign in 1919: Mosley had supported her and spent time in the city campaigning on her behalf.[226]

Curiously, it was the Second World War which revived her reputation. Her husband was elected mayor and she became the city's Mayoress. The war years helped to restore her reputation at least within Plymouth. Her papers also show strenuous efforts in such areas as employing women in the police force. The Chief Constable was against the idea and Lady Astor argued at length to change his opinion.[227] She stood down, unwillingly, from her seat in 1945 and fourteen years later was made an honorary freeman of Plymouth. Lady Astor lived only another five years and she was buried at Cliveden beside Waldorf. Perhaps the most apocryphal story is that of Cliveden, when during breakfast, Lady Astor said to Churchill 'Winston, if I was married to you I'd put poison in your coffee.' He replied: 'Nancy, if I was married to you I'd drink it.'[228]

Dorothy Elmhirst of Dartington Hall

Dorothy Elmhirst had striking similarities and differences with the other American in Devon, Lady Nancy Astor. They were both wealthy heiresses from East Coast society, born in the late nineteenth century and had married Englishmen on their second marriages. Each woman was to have a great impact on Devon but their politics, interests and temperaments were very different.

Their politics were most obviously at variance: Astor's were to the far right whereas Elmhirst was the most visible supporter of the left in Devon. Astor's life was marked by temperance work and a devotion to Christian Science. In America Elmhirst had spent her life pursuing social reform with housing for the poor, education and the women's trade and suffrage movements and later, in England, she continued along similar lines.

Dorothy Whitney was born in Washington D.C. in 1887 to wealthy parents who died when she was young. In 1911, at the age of 24, she married a young banker and diplomat and eventually moved to New York where they had three children. He died at the end of the First World War and seven years later, in 1925, she married Leonard

Dorothy Elmhirst as a young woman

Elmhirst whom she had met when he was a graduate student in New York. That year they discovered Dartington Hall near Totnes and began the work which was to define their lives together.[229] The estate was purchased for some £30,000 and when Dorothy saw it she wrote in her diary 'too heavenly . . . interior difficult!' They crossed the Atlantic to see Dartington together and voyaged on the S.S. *Majestic,* the same ship which had brought Emmeline Pankhurst to Plymouth and where she was arrested in 1913.[230]

Through them the estate was turned over to progressive education and rural regeneration. As a multi-millionaire Dorothy Elmhirst was able to devote considerable sums to fund their endeavours. One of her main interests was in furthering the arts. She backed R. C. Sheriff's play Journey's End in 1928 and the couple partly owned the Globe Theatre and Queen's Theatre in London. In the 1930s Ben and Winifred Nicholson, Henry Moore and Bernard Leach all came to Dartington and refugees arrived who were fleeing the fascists in Germany and Spain. She was also involved in designing the gardens at Dartington.

For some forty years the Elmhirsts were at Dartington. Dorothy Elmhirst died in 1968 and her husband followed six years later. Their ashes were scattered over the garden.[231] Dorothy Elmhirst was an international figure. She had travelled widely before coming to Devon and knew Eleanor and Franklin Roosevelt while living in New York. She remained friendly with them after her second marriage and they shared similar politics.[232] In many ways her legacy remains highly visible in and around Totnes, a town and area with unique characteristics within Devon; the changes originated with the arrival in South Devon of this one woman whom, at her death, was said to be 'one of the most remarkable women of our age'.[233]

In the first years of
the new century

Agatha Christie

Of all Devon's writers Agatha Christie must be the most overwhelmingly popular and resilient. Her life story is probably the most familiar of all the Remarkable Women in this collection. Few Devonians do not know she was born in Torquay, that she had an unhappy first marriage, that she disappeared in what became a national sensation in 1926, that a second marriage proved more fulfilling than her first, and that she achieved extraordinary success in her writing which continued through to her death in 1976. Perhaps it is less known that her father was American and that her mother struggled to maintain what had been a very comfortable lifestyle. Her time in Torquay was formative: First World War service in the Voluntary Aid Detachment as a nurse introduced her to poisons and Belgians. It is assumed Hercule Poirot drew on these memories.[234]

Her first book was published in 1926 and it is easy to find or imagine Devon as a setting in many of those that followed. While writing has formed the mainstay of her reputation it is through their adaption to television and film that continues to bring her to a wide audience. It would be difficult to decide which are the most well-known of her novels: *Murder on the Orient Express* and *Death on the Nile* jostle for preeminence but there is a list of dozens of titles. Personal preferences for actresses playing Miss Marple are as marked as discussions over favourite James Bonds. The extraordinary longevity of 'The Mousetrap' should not be ignored. It has been one of the features of the West End for more than fifty

years. It is remarkable how Christie has carved out a niche in the nation's cultural heritage.

At odds with what is almost a Christie Industry was a woman who kept out of the limelight. The gentility of her settings contrasted with the brutality of murder in the same way as her reluctance to enter the spotlight stands out against the enormity of the Christie legacy. She portrayed murder as normal while she herself maintained a normality of life which was at odds with her celebrity.

The opening of her home of Greenway on the river Dart has reinforced the continued public presence of her and her writing. Although it has been a generation since she died, there appears to be no diminishing in her appeal or importance to Devon.

My Lady of the Moor: Olive Katherine Parr as Beatrice Chase

One of Dartmoor's most famous writers was Olive Katherine Parr, better known under her pseudonym of Beatrice Chase. From 1914 to 1951 she wrote more than twenty novels, a combination of religion and sentiment,[235] although few are read today. [236] Even so her writing and strength of her character made her a notable personality on Dartmoor in the first half of the twentieth century. Although never as popular as Agatha Christie she still registers as one of Devon's leading female writers.

She received the title 'My Lady of the Moor' from the book of that name by John Oxenham (William Arthur Dunkerley who took the name from a character in *Westward Ho!* by Charles Kingsley). Her obituary in *The Times* noted that 'to some she appeared slightly impervious, even awe-inspiring, but others found her easy of approach and a sympathetic companion'. The newspaper also commented that Chase suffered from the popularity of Oxenham's book which resulted in great numbers of visitors to her home at Venton in Widecombe-In-The-Moor. She lived there for 53 years until she died, aged 80, in 1955.[237]

She had a great love of Dartmoor and her concern for it can be found in the pages of *The Times* to which she wrote decrying the use of swaling during the nesting season and of her long campaign to restrict the military use of the moor.[238] It was on Dartmoor that in 1959 a memorial cross was set up. The Campaign Against Cruel Sports donated fifty pounds to it.[239]

Another defining part of her life was a strong sense of religion. This manifested itself in the First World War when she initiated, for soldiers, a Crusade for Chastity. It was during the war that her fiancé died and she never married. Chase created a chapel in her home and called her soldiers 'Knights of the White Crusade'. Its purpose was to instil a 'pure and noble' course of life. She also organised restorative breaks for urban women. Her mother, whom she called 'The Rainbow Maker' because of the coloured glass necklaces she made, sold the jewellery to raise funds for 'poor gentlewomen working in large cities'. The two women turned a nearby cottage into 'St. Michael's Little Home of Rest' where the genteel refugees would stay. Their scheme was extended to two other buildings which were renamed The Anchorage and St Gabriel's.

Towards the end of her life she became more of a recluse, having argued with booksellers she began to sell her own books and postcards direct to visitors. Eventually she resented their intrusion and as her popularity waned so too did her finances. She died in 1955 and was buried in Widecombe churchyard. Chase had wanted to be buried in a field near her home, placed in a open coffin and dressed in a Dominican habit. Only the latter instruction was followed.[240]

Chase had a devotion to animals[241] but as she grew older she appeared to find it difficult to get along with humans and was remembered by one writer as 'a lonely, bitter old woman with a cruel tongue'.[242]

Who was Who in Devonshire in 1934

Seventy-five years ago, in 1934, more than eleven hundred Devonians were selected to appear in *Who's Who in Devonshire*. This was intended to be 'a permanent record of the men and women who have conducted its administrative affairs and taken a prominent part in its religious, professional and business life'.

Less than three percent of them were women: thirty-four women were listed.[243] Nominal descriptions were given of some such as for Lady Georgina Alison of Budleigh Salterton who was noted as being the daughter of one man and the widow of another as was Lady Margaret Maconochie of Seaton. The Hon. Mrs Ida Sebag-Montefiore may also have been included merely because of the circumstances of her birth or marriage but she also had listed her leisure interests of hunting, yachting and walking. The remaining women were more obviously included because of their accomplishments and were leading the way for women in the county.

Half of these thirty-four women were unmarried and ten of remainder were widows. The majority, twenty, were magistrates and had come to the bench in 1920 (2), 1921 (2), 1923 (3), 1924 (4), 1925,

(1), 1926 (1) and 1928 (3). They served the bench for the borough of Barnstaple (Mrs Mary Brannam of Barnstaple), for the borough of Dartmouth (Mrs Maude Hodges of Dartmouth), for Exeter (Dame Audrey Buller of Exeter), for the borough of Plymouth (Miss Elizabeth Bayly of Plymouth) and for the county of Devon (Mrs Mary Baillie of Mortonhampstead, Miss Elsie Batten of Holsworthy, Miss Annie Bazeley of Bideford, Miss Mary Calmady-Hamlyn of Buckfastleigh, Mrs Elizabeth Dashwood of Cullompton, Miss Annie Davie of Bishop's Tawton, Miss Frances Dickinson of Ottery St Mary, Miss Edith Falkner of Ilfracombe, Mrs Margaret Gallup of Brentor, Mrs Amy Kingsford-Lethbridge of Okehampton, Miss Katharine Lazenby of Tiverton, Lady Augusta Peek of Hembury, Mrs Juanita Phillips of Honiton, Mrs Eva Trefusis of Exeter, Miss Eleanor Vicary of Newton Abbot) and for Torquay (Miss Florence Skirrow of Babbacombe). A comparison with lists of all JPs in Devon in the 1920s shows that *Who was Who* omitted some women.[244]

Many of the women had extensive service during the First World War. They included the Honorable Helen Cubitt of Torquay who was Commandant of a convalescent hospital for officers in Torquay for which she was awarded the C.B.E. and Mrs Edith Curzon of Watermouth Castle in Berrynarbor who was given the same award for her convalescent home for wounded British and Belgian soldiers. Another local woman whose war service was recorded was Lady Anne Davy who had served in the Exeter War Hospital and was mentioned in Despatches in 1917. Miss Eleanor Vicary had been a telephone operator, cook and finally quartermaster at the Red Cross Headquarters in France.

Only a few were obviously interested in advancing the interests of other women or at least acknowledged as such in their listed interests. One of them was Miss Florence Skirrow who served for six years as President of the Torquay Branch of the National Council of Women.

Dame Audrey Georgina Buller made an extensive contribution to Devon. She was the youngest daughter of General Sir Redvers Buller and in 1914 she established the Exeter Volunteer Aid Hospital during the First World War. This grew to accommodate 1,500 patients and had 48 auxiliary hospitals affiliated to it. Two years later it was taken over by the War Office but Dame Buller continued as the administrator, the only such post then held by a woman. After the war she served as a county justice. When she died in 1953, Dame Buller was remembered in *The Times* as having 'selfless devotion over many years to the cause of rehabilitating the disabled': this work came from her experiences of seeing men wounded during the war. She established two centres in Surrey and at Exeter (St Loyes). One commentator at the time of her death suggested she had 'the true pioneering spirit'. Dame Buller lived at Bellair, now part of the site for Devon County Hall.[245] What is also interesting about her career, one of the prominent Devon women to first benefit from the right to vote, was that in 1914 she was a member of the National League for Opposing Women's Suffrage.[246]

The public service of Mrs Juanita Maxwell Phillips is impressive. She was born in Valparaiso in Chile in about 1880, married Thomas Phillips, a Honiton solicitor, in 1906 and three years later became a member of the Town Council. She went on to become the town's mayor as well as alderman and was elected to Devon County Council in 1930. She was the first woman to be elected a mayor in Devon (as well as the West Country) and the first to be a county councilor. In addition to this she chaired the Devon Federation of Women's Institutes, a Governor of King's School in Ottery St Mary and Chairman of Honiton Infants' Welfare Clinic. During the First World War she had served in the Accounts Department of the War Office. Her leisure interest was theatre and she had one built in King Street in Honiton. She was awarded an O.B.E. in 1950 and died in 1966, aged 86.[247] Her entry in the *Who was Who* did not mention that she was involved in the vigil for Mrs Pankhurst at Exeter Prison in 1913: she picketed the prison and travelled with Mrs Pankhurst to St David's Station on her release. Every week for several months Mrs Phillips subsequently sold a suffragist paper in the streets of Exeter. She had also presided over the first Suffragist meeting in Honiton, chaired Exeter's branch of the Women's Social and Political Union, and demonstrated in London including at the House of Commons.[248]

There were also three women who were in medicine. Dr Eva Ironside was the Hon. Medical Officer for the Ashburton Cottage Hospital. Miss Jean MacLennan was the Hon. Physician at St Faith's Home for Waifs and Strays in Torquay and had previously worked at the Edinburgh Royal Infirmary, the Jenny Lind Hospital for Children in Norwich and the Bristol Royal Infirmary. By 1926 Gwendolyn Rolfe was Medical Officer at the Exeter Dispensary and had already worked at the Royal Devon & Exeter Hospital as well as at the Royal Isle of Wight County Hospital.

One of the more unusual life histories was that of Miss Annie Bazeley of Bideford. She served in various public roles in the town both before and after the First World War but it is her work during the war itself that was unusual. She had served as a Voluntary Aid Detachment nurse in Devon and then as an Examiner in postal censorship in Germany from 1918 to 1919. Then, from 1923 to 1924 she worked as a policewoman in the W.A.S. in Cologne with the Army of Occupation.

Although women feature spectacularly poorly in numerical terms, the list of Who was Who shows what women were becoming capable of being and becoming by the early 1930s.

Women at work on the Home Front in the Second World War

Women in 1940 and 1941 were implored to keep the country going. Local newspapers were full of stories showing how women were taking up the tasks left behind by the men fighting overseas. Devon women did their share and were involved in a variety of

Taxi drivers in Torquay

occupations which might have been surprising then but would now seem ordinary to modern society.

Their work brought out a debate over the wearing of trousers. Women in Civil Defence work in Plymouth had to choose between skirts or slacks as their uniform. Seventy-five per cent chose skirts because they were thought more feminine. Most of them were older women who would not wear slacks. One woman said she preferred

Plymouth bus conductors

Patrolling Dartmoor

them for 'utility and comfort' but they were an innovation many did not think suited women. However, one practical woman said:

'They give better freedom of movement if ladders have to be climbed or debris scrambled over. In such circumstances skirts would prove and be a real nuisance. From the personal comfort angle slacks are warmer than skirts and effect economy and stockings. A woman can even wear laddered stockings with trousers and does not let her sex down'.

Scanning the skies of Dartmoor

For other women the wearing of skirts was not a problem. The one hundred female bus conductors at Plymouth had smart alpaca uniforms with skirts and, according to one journalist, used 'a dash of lipstick' to give them confidence. They were 'doing a man's job, drawing a man's pay, and the money they earn is going, in many cases, to eke out a sadly depleted family budget'. Others were saving money so they could marry.

Women helping the Home Guard on Dartmoor had different clothes altogether. A mounted patrol of women observers was formed at Yelverton and ranged the moor in pairs watching the skies. There had been objections from men when the idea was first suggested but by the summer of 1940 there were twenty women in the section. They ranged from 16 years old to nearly 60 and worked four hour shifts from 5.30 in the morning until 9 at night. They wore riding kit with white armlets on which were written 'Mounted Patrol, LDV'.

Women were also driving taxis in Devon. Nine women worked for one firm in Plymouth. Most of them were married and worked from seven in the morning until five at night. They wore peak caps and blue cotton coats which one woman said 'we like the peak caps. They're smart and we're allowed to use a reasonable amount of make-up'. Another admitted her new work was much more interesting than housework which she found tedious. There were also women driving taxis in Paignton.

Torquay also had women gardeners. A dancer and a former London mannequin worked in khaki dungarees. Both women had their careers interrupted by the war, joined the Land Army and were sent to Torquay. One said 'it isn't like manual labour, lifting weights or anything' and thought it was a perfect job for women who could do it just as efficiently as a man.

Perhaps most surprising of all were the 'Women Guerillas' at Plymouth. In April 1942 nearly twenty women began training in hand grenade and musketry drill. Each woman was a Civil Defence Warden and one said 'we are quite prepared to tackle Tommy Guns, if they give us the chance'.

It had been announced that Civil Defence workers were being allowed to train as a special Home Guard section. Miss F. Julian Smith suggested 'and why not the women as well?' The best bomb-throwers were said to be able to hit targets at 25 to 30 feet. One of the male wardens said 'They are real Amazons, ready to tackle anything'. There was also a second group of women doing similar training in Plymouth. One of them wrote 'whilst it is hoped that

Painting for the blackout

149

Plymouth salvage workers

they will not find it necessary to put the training into actual practice they believe in being prepared'. They, or possibly a third group, were based at Mutley Baptist Church, and were an unofficial group who received training once a week. They worked as clerks during the day. One of them said 'Stories of the Russian women guerillas made us feel we wanted to be prepared. I think everyone should know how to handle a gun'.[249]

The times made these women appear to be remarkable when in fact they were always of carrying out these duties but not allowed to do so. What is remarkable is that once the war was over these jobs were again largely denied to these women.

Conclusion: a grandmother's advice from 1918

Perhaps a fitting last word would be the advice given by a grandmother at the end of the First World War. This unidentified woman was born in about 1843 and aged 75 years old when interviewed by a journalist for the *Exeter Flying Post* in 1918.[250] He reported that 'Grandmother sincerely pities the young folks of this early Twentieth Century and that for a quaint reason which has nothing to do with the world tragedy of the past four years.' She had told him:

'With all your modern advantages that we hear so much about I wouldn't have your youth in exchange for mine that ended fifty years ago. We worked hard and long hours then, it is true, and we had few pleasures. But we did the first conscientiously because it was the business of our lives and we enjoyed the last because of their rarity. When you come to be seventy-odd –if ever you live to, with the pace you're going at, especially now that air travel is coming in – if you live to be seventy-odd, you'll miss what is the greatest pleasure of my old age – looking back upon a placid, pleasant youth that is restful to remember. Your memories, I should think, will be like looking back at one of those scurrying cinema pictures, you're so fond of going to, and they'll give your old heads an ache to think of'.

The oldest people living today would be the generation that she was cautioning. The journalist pointed out that many modern conveniences had not been known in her youth such as motor cars, electricity and moving pictures but that they shared gas and locomotives. Even so, the older woman pointed out that in her youth people did not rush as much: her first journey to London took eleven hours on the train. Also, fashions did not alter as quickly and she stressed clothes lasted a generation. Her thoughts on shopping are equally unfamiliar: shop owners would, she said, provide lunch for favourite customers in their homes which were above the stores.

Although her comments were made within living memory modern life has dramatically altered since then. Over that time radio, television, computers and the internet have revolutionised life. Her generation of women had yet to vote in national elections and those at home had yet to experience the washing machine, a technological invention which arguably was one of the most important of the twentieth century. What remains the same however, is trying to understand the changes in one's own lifetime and of those that precipitated it in the generations before. She spoke just as women were being given the right to vote and when activists were demanding that men and women should receive equal pay when doing comparable jobs. In many ways her time is unknown to us but in other ways, some surprising, it is all too familiar.

Notes

1   For instance, see Tristram Risdon, *The Chorographical Description or Survey of the county of Devon* (1811), 9-12.

2   John Prince, *The Worthies of Devon* (1810 edn).

3   Devon Record Office, Z19/7/7.

4   The preface to the 1810 edition failed to notice any omission.

5   William Chapple (ed.), *A Review of Part of Risdon's Survey of Devon* (Exeter, 1785), 35.

6   *Story of the Women's Window in the Cathedral Church of St Peter* (Exeter, no date given), 5-6.

7   Exceptions include Margarita Rendel, 'Women in Torquay in the first half of the nineteenth century', *Devonshire Association Transactions*, vol. 126, 1994, 17-39; Lynne Mayers, *Bal Maidens* (Blaize Bailey Books, 2008) and *A Dangerous place to work!* (Blaize Bailey Books, 2008); *Jobs for the Girls? stories of local women and work* (Plymouth, 2001).

8   It was only in 2006 that Elizabeth Crawford's *The Women's Suffrage Movement in Britain and Ireland; A Regional Survey* appeared. This includes a section on Devon. Just as this book was going to print Margarita Rendel's article on the women's suffrage movement in Devon has been published in the *Transactions of the Devonshire Association*, volume 140, 2008.

9   The figures have been taken from the summaries of the censuses held within the parliamentary papers at the House of Commons.

10   Karen Levitan, 'Redundancy, the 'Surplus Woman' problem and the British Census, 1851–1861', *Women's History Review*, Vol. 17, No. 3, July 2008, 359-60.

11   Devon Record Office, Z19/1/16.

12   John Watkins, *An essay towards a history of Bideford* (Exeter, 1792), 46-7.

13   Jennifer Clarke, *Exploring the West Country, a woman's guide* (1987), 62.

14   *Women's Herald*, 20 February 1892, Issue 173.

15   *Torquay Times*, 20 October 1922.

16   Todd Gray (ed.), *Devon household accounts, 1627–59, Part 2: Henry, fifth Earl of Bath, and Rachel, Countess of Bath, of Tawstock and London, 1637–1655* , Devon and Cornwall Record Society, NS 39 (1996).

17   Caroline M. K. Bowden, 'Lady Rachel, Countess of Bath', *Dictionary of National Biography*.

18   Gray, *Devon household accounts, 1627–59, Part 2: Henry, fifth Earl of Bath, and Rachel, Countess of Bath, of Tawstock and London, 1637–1656.*

19   Devon Record Office, 2723M/SF15. I am grateful to Sue Laithwaite for drawing my attention to this collection.

20   Ursula Radford, 'Miss Burney in Devonshire', *Transactions of the Devonshire Association,* LIX, 1927, 288.

21   Edmund Butcher, The Beauties of Sidmouth Displayed (Sidmouth, no date given), 12. I am grateful to Bernard Hallen for this reference.

22   British Library, Additional Manuscript 28793.

23   The Early Diary of Frances Burney, 1776–1778 (1907), I, 212.

24   The Early Diary, 21.

25   The Early Diary, 21.

26   The Works of Augustus Toplady (1825), I, 137-8.

27   Devon Record Office, 564M/F8 edited in Todd Gray, *Travels In Georgian Devon* (Tiverton, 1998), II, 157.

28   The Early Diary, 21.

29   Devon Record Office, 564M/F2 edited in Todd Gray, *Travels In Georgian Devon* (Tiverton, 1997), I, 75.

30   British Library, Additional Manuscript 28793.

31   The Early Diary, 21.

32   British Library, Additional Manuscript 28793.

33   Jack Simmons, *A Devon Anthology* (1970), 132. They were still doing it in 1807: Exeter Flying Post, 24 September 1807.

34   *Exeter Flying Post,* 2 September 1885.

35   Todd Gray, *Devon Household Accounts, 1627-59,* I, Devon & Cornwall Record Society, 1995, Vol. 38, xxxii-xxxvii, 1-110.

36   Todd Gray, *Exeter Unveiled* (Exeter, 2003), 65-7.

37   F. T. Elworthy, 'The Exmoor Scolding', *Transactions of the Devonshire Association,* 1880, vol. 12, 483-9; T. N. Brushfield, 'Who wrote the Exmoor Scolding and Courtship', *Transactions of the Devonshire Association,* 1888, vol. 20, 400-409.

38   *Brice's Weekly Journal,* 2 June 1727.

39   There were eighteenth-century editions published in 1750, 1768, 1771, 1775, 1782, 1788, 1794 and 1796.

40   Devon Record Office, CC5/403.

41   Devon Record Office, CC5/347.

42   Devon Record Office, CC5/160.

43   The collection is a rich source of information but was severely damaged in the bombing of Exeter in May 1942 and many documents are unavailable for public examination.

44   Ian Maxted, 'Andrew Brice', *Dictionary of National Biography.*

45   Anne McTaggart, *Memoirs of a Gentlewoman of the Old School* (1830), I, 26-73.

46   *The Examiner,* 2 January 1825.

47   *Exeter Flying Post,* 29 October 1873.

48   *The Examiner,* 2 January 1825.

49   *The Examiner,* 2 January 1825.

50   Joseph Knight, rev. K. D. Reynolds, 'Maria Foote', *Dictionary of National Biography*.

51   Sabine Baring Gould, *Devonshire Characters and Strange Events* (1926 edn), 23.

52   Baring Gould, *Devonshire Characters and Strange Events*, 31.

53   Joseph Knight, rev. K. D. Reynolds, 'Maria Foote', *Dictionary of National Biography*.

54   *The Belfast Newsletter*, Issue 34048, 22 January 1868.

55   *The Leeds Mercury*, 7 January 1868.

56   Devon Record Office, 564M/F7, edited in Todd Gray, *Travels in Georgian Devon* (Tiverton, 1998), II, 103; R. B. M., 'A Scotswoman on Devon, 1803', *Devon & Cornwall Notes & Queries*, Volume 16, 316.

57   R. B. M., 'Budleigh Salterton and General Simcoe', *Devon & Cornwall Notes & Queries*, Volume 16, 230.

58   R. B. M., 'A Scotswoman on Devon, 1803', *Devon & Cornwall Notes & Queries*, Volume 16, 316.

59   Devon Record Office, 1038 M/F.

60   *Gentleman's Magazine*, June 1817, 492.

61   *Bristol Journal*, 4 March 1797.

62   R. N. Worth cited by Lois Lamplugh in *A History of Ilfracombe* (Chichester, 1984), 30.

63   W. S. Lack-Szyrma, 'The Red Cloaks and British Soldiers', *The Western Antiquary*, July – August 1890, vol. X, no. 1, 112 and 'The Red Cloak Traditions', *The Western Antiquary*, vol. XI, 141; Arthur Mee, 'The Red Cloak Traditions', *The Western Antiquary*, vol. X, 169.

64   *My Miscellanies* (1863). It had been originally published four years earlier.

65   *The Scientific Magazine*, 1797, Vol. 1, 209.

66   C. Stuart, *A history of all the real and threatened invasions of England from the landing of Julius Caesar to the present* (Windsor, 1798), 199.

67   *Western Morning News*, 6 February 1935.

68   Daniel and Samuel Lysons, *Magna Britannia . . . Devon* (1822), vii-viii.

69   Percy Russell, *Dartmouth* (1950), 46; A. M. Jackson, 'Letter from a Breton Knight', *Devon & Cornwall Notes & Queries* (1970), vol. 31, 216-218.

70   Tristram Risdon, *The Chorographical description or survey of the county of Devon* (1714), 61.

71   Martin Dunsford, *Historical Memoirs of the Town and Parish of Tiverton* (Tiverton, 1790), 169.

72   R. N. Worth, *A History of Devonshire* (1895), 285.

73   Dunsford, *Tiverton*, 241.

74   Dunsford, *Tiverton*, 247.

75   *Freeman's Journal and Daily Commercial Advertiser*, 13 March 1894.

76   Andrew Elfenbein, 'Lesbian Aestheticism on the Eighteenth-Century Stage', *Eighteenth-Century Life*, Vol. 25, No. 1, Winter 2001, 1-16.

77   *The Ladies' Treasury*, 1 October 1895; Thomas Moore, *The History of Devonshire* (no date given), 832-4.

78   Mary de la Mahotière, 'Hannah Cowley', *Dictionary of National Biography*; *The Examiner*, 26 March 1809; *The Morning Chronicle*, 23 March 1809.

79   Nicole Pohl, *Women, Space and Utopia, 1600 – 1800* (2006), 80.

80   Kaye Bagshaw, 'Jane Parminter', *Dictionary of National Biography*; Lynne Walker, 'The entry of women into the architectural profession', *Women's Art Journal*, vol. 7, no. 1, (Spring – Summer 1986), 13-14.

81   Kaye Bagshaw, 'Jane Parminter', *Dictionary of National Biography*; Lynne Walker, 'The entry of women into the architectural profession', *Women's Art Journal*, vol. 7, no. 1, (Spring – Summer 1986), 13-14.

82   Robert Michael Smith, 'The London Jew Society and Patterns of Jewish Conversion in England, 1801 – 1859', *Jewish Social Studies*, vol. 43, no. 3/4, (Summer – Autumn, 1981), 277.

83   Kaye Bagshaw, 'Jane Parminter', *Dictionary of National Biography*.

84   Sylvia Bowerbank, 'Joanna Southcott', *Dictionary of National Biography*.

85   *Exeter Flying Post*, 8 September 1814.

86   Sylvia Bowerbank, 'Joanna Southcott', *Dictionary of National Biography*.

87   *Exeter Flying Post*, 8 December 1814.

88   *The Examiner*, 24 September 1809; *The Universal Magazine*, September 1814.

89   Sylvia Bowerbank, 'Joanna Southcott', *Dictionary of National Biography*.

90   *Exeter Flying Post*, 5 January 1815.

91   Sylvia Bowerbank, 'Joanna Southcott', *Dictionary of National Biography*.

92   Sarah Catherine Martin, *The comic adventures of old mother Hubbard and her dog* (1805).

93   Plymouth & West Devon Record Office, 74/572/4. This account is dated 1913.

94   It was in print by the spring of 1799 in *Dr Arnold's New Juvenile Amusements*: *The Times*, 17 April 1799.

95   For instance see John Dryden, *The Hind and the Panther a poem* (1687); Thomas Nashe, *Strange Newes of the intercepting certain letters and a convoy of verses as they were going privily to victual the Low Countries* (1592). Also, in 1751 John Winstanley's *Poems Written Occasionally by the Late John Winstanley* included Part of Mother Hubbard's Tale.

96   *The Ipswich Journal*, 14 December 1805; *Liverpool Mercury*, 25 January 1822.

97   *Exeter Flying Post*, 1 February 1863; *Penny Illustrated*, 11 February 1863; *The Lady's Newspaper*, 16 May 1863; *The Times*, 13 May 1863..

98   *Exeter Flying Post*, 26 August 1858; *Western Times*, 21 August 1858.

99   *Exeter Flying Post*, 2 August 1855.

100   *The Morning Chronicle*, 3 September 1859; *Birmingham Post*, 24 August 1859.

101   *Bristol Mercury*, 16 September 1854.

102   *Liverpool Mercury*, 25 April 1870.

103   *Exeter Flying Post*, 6 September 1855.

104   June A. Sheppard, 'Brighton's railway workers in the 1850s', *Sussex Archaeological Collections*, vol. 139, 2001, 193.

105   C. H. Cooper, 'Mrs Partington', *Notes and Queries*, No. 57, November 30 1850, 447.

106   Ronald J. Zboray and Mary Saracino Zboray, 'Gender Slurs in Boston's Partisan Press During the 1840s', *Journal of American Studies* (2000), 34, 413-46.

107   Anna Sutton, *A Story of Sidmouth* (1953), 38; Westcountry Studies Library,

Peter Orlando Hutchinson, *A History of Sidmouth*, III, 150. Hutchinson does not mention Mrs Partington.

108 C. H. Cooper, 'Mrs Partington', *Notes and Queries*, No. 57, November 30 1850, 447.

109 Robert Cole, 'Mrs Partington', *Notes and Queries*, No. 55, November 16 1850, 409.

110 *The Taunton Courier*, 12 October 1831, reprinted in the *Cambridge History of English and American Literature* (1907-21), vol. xvi.

111 Bodleian Library, John Johnson collection of cartoons, 24 October 1831.

112 Todd Gray, *Lost Devon* (Exeter, 2003), 130-1.

113 See *The Age*, 6 March 1836, 77; *John Bull*, 23 March 1844; *Cleave's Penny Gazette*, 3 February 1838, issue 17; *The Age*, 27 September 1840, 308; *John Bull*, 20 August 1843, 537.

114 She was mentioned in debates on 15 March 1991 and 4 October 2001.

115 Todd Gray (ed.), *East Devon, the Travellers' Tales* (Exeter, 2000), 159.

116 'John Rolle', J. M. Rigg, revised by Roland Thorne, *Dictionary of National Biography*.

117 *Exeter Flying Post*, 25 November 1885.

118 Elizabeth Howard, *The Hon. Mark Rolle* (Downham Market, 2007), 1-2.

119 *The World*, 9 December 1885.

120 David Mead, *Bicton Park, Botanical Gardens* (Bicton, 2001), 20-1.

121 M. A. Wilson, 'Amelia Warren Griffiths of Torquay—a pioneer botanist', *Transactions and Proceedings for 1951–52, Torquay Natural History Society*, 11/2 (1953), 74–7

122 Ann B. Shteir, 'Amelia Griffiths', *Dictionary of National Biography*; Wilson, 'Amelia Warren Griffiths of Torquay—a pioneer botanist', 74–7.

123 *The Illustrated Household Journal and Englishwoman's Domestic Magazine*, 1 September 1881.

124 Monypenny, *Life of Disraeli* (1912), 36.

125 Harwick, *Mrs Dizzy*, 160.

126 Hardwick, *Mrs Dizzy*, 152.

127 Jane Ridley, 'Mary Anne Disraeli', *Dictionary of National Biography*.

128 James Sykes, Mary Anne Disraeli (1928), 17-19; Mollie Hardwick, *Mrs Dizzy, the life of Mary Anne Disraeli, Viscountess Beaconsfield* (1972), 10, 160.

129 Harwick, *Miss Dizzy*, 6.

130 Jane Ridley, 'Mary Anne Disraeli', *Dictionary of National Biography*.

131 They returned in September 1854, August 1855, September 1856, November 1857, September and December 1858, November 1859, January 1861 and 24 December 1862: Exeter Flying Post, 18 & 25 August 1853, 14 September 1854, 16 August 1855, 25 September 1856, 26 November 1857, 23 September 1858, 2 December 1858, 17 November 1859, 2 January 1861, 24 December 1862.

132 Monypenny, *The Life of Benjamin Disraeli*, 461.

133 Monypenny, *The Life of Benjamin Disraeli*, 453.

134 Monypenny, *The Life of Benjamin Disraeli*, 454.

135 Monypenny, *The Life of Benjamin Disraeli*, 463.

136 M. G. Wiebe, 'Mrs Sarah Brydges Willyams', *Dictionary of National Biography*.
137 *Exeter Flying Post*, 20 April 1864.
138 *The Englishwoman's Review*, 14 January 1888, CLXXVI.
139 The others were in Wales and London: *The Englishwoman's Review*, 14 January 1888, CLXXVI.
140 Ellen Jordan, 'The great principle of English fair-play: male champions, the English women's movement and the admission of women to the pharmaceutical society in 1879', *Women's History Review*, 1998, 7:3, 381-410.
141 *Chemist and Druggist*, 1892, 143-4.
142 Information supplied by the Royal Pharmaceutical Society Museum.
143 Information supplied by the Royal Pharmaceutical Society Museum.
144 *The Monthly Packet of Evening Readings for Members of the English Church*, 1 October 1879, p.408, Issue 166.
145 The eleventh report of the House of Rest, along with some other papers, is housed at Manchester Central Library, M50/5, 27/4.
146 *The Girl's Own Paper*, 7 May 1898, Issue 958, page 501
147 *Torquay Times*, 1 June 1900.
148 *The Girl's Own Paper*, 7 May 1898, Issue 958, page 501.
149 *Torquay Times*, 1 June 1900.
150 Her association with the House of Rest is mentioned in the *Women's Union Journal*, 15 November 1889, and in the Eleventh Report housed at Manchester Central Library.
151 *Liverpool Mercury*, 2 September 1881.
152 She had been living in Torquay and died in November 1888. She was buried in Torquay: Eric Richards, 'George Granville Leveson Gower', *Dictionary of National Biography*.
153 *Birmingham Daily Post*, 3 April 1889.
154 *The Monthly Packet of Evening Readings for Members of the English Church*, 1 January 1880, p103, Issue 169.
155 *Torquay Times*, 1 June 1900.
156 October 01, 1879; 29 January 1889; 16 August 1895; September 1880; June 1887; 2 September 1881.
157 The article is undated and appeared in an unknown issue on page 33.
158 Maude Stanley, *Clubs for Working Girls* (Edinburgh, 1890), 93.
159 It appeared in an unknown issue on page 22.
160 The *Torquay Directory* recorded a change in the issue of 14 September 1887. Ferny Hollow was advertised for sale in 1888: *Torquay Directory*, 21 March 1888.
161 *Torquay Times*, 15 June 1900.
162 *Murray's Magazine*, June 1887.
163 *Torquay Directory*, 23 October 1918 & 18 October 1922.
164 *Kelly's Directory for Devon* (1939).
165 *www.bbc.co.uk/ww2peopleswar/stories/59/a4176759.shtm*.
166 *Torquay Times*, 22 January & 5 March 1971.
167 Alston Kennerley, *Dictionary of National Biography*.
168 Weston, *Life*, 64-5.

169 Weston, *Life*, 81.
170 Weston, *Life*, 82.
171 Weston, *Life*, 279-80.
172 *The Times*, 28 October 1918.
173 *The Times*, 1 November 1918.
174 Weston, *Life*, 392.
175 For a discussion of the term see Laura E. Nym Mayhall, 'Defining Militancy: Radical protest, the constitutional idiom and women's suffrage in Britain, 1908 to 1909', *The Journal of British Studies*, Vol. 39, No. 3, July 2000, 340-71.
176 Laura E. Nym Marshall, *The Militant Suffrage Movement* (Oxford, 2003), 60-1
177 Royal College of Physicians London, memoirs of Mabel Ramsay, 116.
178 *Western Morning News*, 15 January 1930.
179 Royal College of Physicians London, memoirs of Mabel Ramsay, 116.
180 *Western Daily Mercury*, 4 April 1913.
181 Juliet Gardner, *The Guardian*, 14 March 2003.
182 Purvis, *Emmeline Pankhurst*, 101; Crawford, *The Women's Suffrage Movement*, 8, 239. Afterwards Mrs Gawthorpe and Mrs Pankhurst campaigned against Winston Churchill in the Dundee by-election.
183 Women's Library, TWL.2004.548. She had the support of Selina Cooper, Mrs Strachey, Edith Palliser and E. M. Gardner.
184 Antonia Raeburn, *The Militant Suffragettes* (Newton Abbot, 1974), 45.
185 *The Times*, 16 December 1907, 1, 6, 8, 10 and 20 January 1908; Crawford, *The Women's Suffrage Movement*, 146; Purvis, *Emmeline Pankhurst*, 101-102; Raeburn, *The Militant Suffragettes*, 45-6.
186 Philip Carter, *Newton Abbot* (Exeter, 2004), 108-109.
187 *The Times*, 21 January 1908.
188 *The Times*, 6 August 1913 & 12 July 1922; *North Devon Journal*, 7 August 1913.
189 *North Devon Journal*, 25 June 1914.
190 Raeburn, *The Militant Suffragettes*, 99-100.
191 Raeburn, *The Militant Suffragettes*, 100; *North Devon Journal*, 3 June 1909.
192 *The Times*, 2 August 1909; Bradley, *Cornwall*, 47; Crawford, *The Woman's Suffrage Movement*, 133, 144.
193 *The Torquay Directory*, 18 August 1909.
194 *The Times*, 2 August 1909.
195 *Exeter Flying Post*, 10 May 1913; Bradley, *Cornwall*, 47-8.
196 *Exeter Flying Post*, 31 July & 7 August 1909.
197 *Western Daily Mercury*, 28 June 1913.
198 *Western Morning News*, 15 January 1930; Katherine Bradley, *Cornwall*, 65-9; Western Daily Mercury, 27 June 1913.
199 Royal College of Physicians of London, Dr Ramsay's memoirs, 117-118.
200 *Exeter Flying Post*, 5 July 1913; *Western Times*, 24 June 1913.
201 *Western Morning News*, 16 December 1929; *The Times*, 5 December 1913.
202 *Western Daily Mercury*, 4 December 1913.
203 Purvis, *Emmeline Pankhurst* (2002), 240.
204 *Exeter Flying Post*, 6 December 1913; *Western Daily Mercury*, 6 December 1913.

205 *The Times,* 5 December 1913; *Western Daily Mercury,* 6 December 1913.

206 *Exeter Flying Post,* 13 December 1913.

207 Purvis, *Emmeline Pankhurst,* 240.

208 *Exeter Flying Post,* 13 December 1913; *The Times,* 16 December 1913.

209 June Purvis, *Emmeline Pankhurst* (2002), 272.

210 *The Times,* 11 May 1954.

211 These are now housed at the Royal College of Physicians of London. Excerpts were published in *The Western Evening Herald* from 16 August 1978 to 22 September 1978.

212 She qualified MD Ed 1912; MBChB 1906; FRCS Ed 1921; MRCOG 1929. The 1901 census lists her as a boarder in Edinburgh, aged 22, and notes she was born in 'about 1879'.

213 See Mabel L. Ramsay and H. F. Vellacott, 'Hydatid Cysts of Liver', British Medical Journal, 3 February 1923, 184-5.

214 Mabel L. Ramsay and Florence A. Stoney, 'Anglo-French Hospital, No. 2, Chateau Tourlaville, Cherbourg', *British Medical Journal,* 5 June 1915, 966-9.

215 'Medical women and the Post Office', *British Medical Journal,* 18 May 1929, 929.

216 *The Times,* 11 May 1954.

217 Plymouth & West Devon Record Office, 682.

218 The early records were destroyed in the bombing at Plymouth: Plymouth & West Devon Record Office, 832/10.

219 Linda Gilroy said 'Plymouth's medical women played a significant role in the services. Eight of them, trained under pioneer nurse Priscilla Sellon, worked with Florence Nightingale in the Crimea, and pioneer woman surgeon Dr. Mabel Ramsey worked on the battlefields in the First World War': Hansard Debates, 17 October 1997, part 27.

220 Plymouth & West Devon Record Office, 2614/1.

221 *Express & Echo,* 4, 6, 7, 9 & 13 September 1918.

222 Martin Pugh, 'Nancy Astor', *Dictionary of National Biography.*

223 *Western Morning News,* 15 January 1930.

224 Royall College of Physicians of London, memoirs of Dr Ramsay, 113-114.

225 Martin Pugh, 'Nancy Astor', *Dictionary of National Biography;* Karen J. Musolf, *From Plymouth to Parliament* (1999), 160-64; Anthony Masters, *Nancy Astor, a life* (1981).

226 Todd Gray, *Blackshirts In Devon* (Exeter, 2006), 37-8, 41.

227 Plymouth & West Devon Record Office, 186/20/65.

228 Martin Pugh, 'Nancy Astor', *Dictionary of National Biography.*

229 Lottie Hoare, 'Dorothy Elmhirst', *Dictionary of National Biography.*

230 Michael Young, *The Elmhirsts of Dartington* (1982), 107; The Times, 16 September 1983.

231 Lottie Hoare, 'Dorothy Elmhirst', *Dictionary of National Biography.*

232 James Leutze, 'The secret of the Churchill-Roosevelt Correspondence: September 1939 – May 1940, *Journal of Contemporary History,* vol. 10, no. 3, July 1975, 480-1.

233 *The Times,* 18 December 1968.

234 Janet Morgan, 'Agatha Christie', *Dictionary of National Biography*.

235 *The Times*, 5 July 1955.

236 *The Heart of the Moor* (1914), *Through a Dartmoor Window* (1915), Pearl (1919), *Complete tales of my Knights and Ladies* (1919), *Pages of Peace from Dartmoor* (1920), *The Dartmoor Window Again* (1921), *Lady Agatha, A Romance of Tintagel* (1922), *Lady Avis Trewithen, A Romance of Dartmoor* (1922), *A Dartmoor Galahad* (1923), *Devon and Heaven* (1924), *The Voice of the River* (1925), *The Cry for a Heart* (1925), *A White-handed Saint* (c.1925), *Patricia Lancaster's Revenge* (1928), *The Twelfth, An Amethyst* (1929), *Dartmoor Snapshots* (1931), *The Passing of the Rainbow Maker* (1939), *The Corpse on the Moor* (1946), *The Dartmoor Window Forty Years After* (1948), *Dartmoor The Beloved* (1951).

237 *The Times*, 5 July 1955.

238 *The Times*, 1 May 1924 & 1 January 1947.

239 *The Times*, 15 July 1959.

240 Christina Green, *Beatrice Chase, My Lady of the Moor* (Dawlish, 1974); Beatrice Chase, *The Passing of the Rainbow Maker* (Bristol, 1926); Judy Chard, *The Mysterious Lady of the Moor* (Chudleigh,1994).

241 One of her publications was *A Future Life for Loving Animals*.

242 Green, *Beatrice Chase*, 14.

243 *Who's who in Devonshire* (Hereford, 1934), preface, 8, 13, 19, 20, 31, 36, 41, 68, 69, 70, 71, 73, 88, 97, 126, 134, 146, 153, 159, 165, 192, 205, 206, 208, 225, 236, 242, 265, 267, 270, 275.

244 For instance there were a considerably larger number of female JPs in 1923 and 1935. In 1923 there were 12 female JPs, many of them do not feature in the later *Who was Who*: *Kelly's Directories for Devon* (1923, 1935 edns).

245 *The Times*, 23 & 27 June 1953.

246 *Exeter Flying Post*, 7 March 1914.

247 Cheryl Law, *Women: A Modern Political Dictionary* (2000), 122-3; *The Times*, 16 November 1966; *Express & Echo*, 16 November 1966. *Kelly's Directory for Devonshire* in 1935 lists Mrs Philips and Mrs H. M. Clifford as county councillors. Mrs Phillips was elected first: Devon Record Office: 148/39.

248 *Express & Echo*, 18 March 1930.

249 See for instance, *Western Morning News*, 9 July 1940, 25 July 1940, 17 January 1941, 7 June 1942, 3 August 1942, 20 December 1942.

250 *Exeter Flying Post*, 14 December 1918.

Index

Adams, Miriam 6-7
A-La-Ronde 55-6
Alison, Georgina 142
Amazons 14-19, 51, 149
Arnold, Samuel 59
Ashburton 6-7
Asquith, Arthur 113; Herbert 110,
    113-115
Astor, Nancy 2, 126, 132-5; Waldorf
    133-4
Australia 111
Awliscombe 44-8

Baillie, Mary 143
Barnstaple 12, 43
Bastard, John Pollexfen 59
Bath 79, 99
Batten, Elsie 143
Bazeley, Annie 143, 145
Bentinck, Lady 114
Berkeley, William 43
Berry Pomeroy 89
Berrynarbor 143
Besant, Walter 93-4
Bethel movement 102
Bicton 77-80
Bideford 114; Pavilion 113
Bishop's Tawton 143
Bishopsteignton 7
Blackpool 51
Bolt, Mr 73
Bourchier, Henry 9-11; Rachel 9-12
Brampford Speke 83

Brandon, family 20
Brannan, Mary 143
Brentor 143
Brice, Andrew 25-7, Sarah 27
Brighton 71
Bristol 115, 117; Cliveden 135
Brooke, Christian 26
Bryant, Private G. 127
Buckfastleigh 143
Buckingham, Elizabeth 51
Budleigh Salterton 119, 142
Buller, Audrey 143-4; Redvers 143
Burges, Mary Anne 44-8, 55
Burney, Fanny 14-19; Maria 14-15
Burrit, Elihu 77-8
Burrowes, Jane 26
Bus conductors 146, 148

Calmady-Hamlyn, Mary 143
Canada, Newfoundland 13, 14-15, 45;
    Quebec 70
Carlisle 81
Carrington, Earl 115
Charles I, 11, 20
Charlotte, Queen 44
Chase, Beatrice 140-2
Chastity Crusade 141
Christie, Agatha 2, 138-9
Christmas 11, 59
Churchill, Winston 109, 135
Clannaborough 26
Clarendon 11
Clay-cutters 111-112

Cloaks 49-50
Clovelly Court 110, 113-115
Collins, Wilkie 49
Commins, Mary 24
Cook, Beryl 3
Coombe Cellars 16
Cornwall 49; Land's End 118; St Issey 81; Torpoint 118; Truro 71
Cowley, Hannah 53-4
Craik, Diana Marie 97-8
Cranfield, Lionel 9-10
Crediton 26
Crone, Isaac 67-9
Cross-dressing 67-72
Crosse, Mary Anne 24
Cubitt, Helen 143
Cullompton 143
Curzon, Edith 143

Dartington Hall 136-7
Dartmoor 20, 52, 121, 140-2, 147
Dartmouth 45-6, 51, 143
Dashwood, Elizabeth 143
Davie, Annie 143
Dawkins, Margery 36
de Rothschild, Madame Lionel 87-8
Deluc, Jean Andre 44
Devonport 102-7, 122-3; Ford Hospital 127-30
Dickinson, Frances 143
Disraeli, Benjamin 82-9; Mary Anne 82-8
Dogs 87-8
Drake, Sir Francis 23-4
Drummond Castle 88
Dunkerly, William Arthur 140
Durham 91

Easterling, Ruth 4
Edwards, Susannah 6
Eller, Mary 26
Ellis, Agnes 26
Elmhirst, Dorothy 2, 135-7; Leonard 135-7
Emigration 5
Evans , Eleanor 83; family 82-4; John 83; Mary 2, 82-9
Exeter 20, 23-4, 25-7, 38-40, 52, 56,

67-8, 79, 85, 124, 143; Acland Arms 82-3, 85; Belgrave Road 117; Bellair 144; bishop 58; cathedral 4, 39; Exe Island 117; Fore Street 119; Gervase Avenue 119; Great Western Hotel 122; Guildhall 67-70; hospital 143-4; Old Vicarage Road 131; prison 115-117, 121; Rougemont Hotel 117; Royal Clarence Hotel 40; St Loyes 144; St Thomas 131-2; Sidwell Street 82-3, 85; South Street 119; The Mint 82; Victoria Hall 115
Exmoor 25-38
Exmouth 65-6, 77, 79, 119

Falkner, Edith 143
Fane, Anthony 9; Rachel see Bourchier
Fascism 134
Fawcett, Millicent 122, 125
Fish 13-18, 20, 21, 67, 88
Flannel 66
Foote, Maria 2, 40-3; Mrs 40-1; Samuel T. 40
Fortnum & Mason 86
France 49-51, 125, 127
Fraser, Elsie 127-30
Frogwell, Dick 30
Fuller, Bishop 58
Fursdon, Henry 30
Furse, George 29-30, 31; Tom 34

Gallup, Margaret 143
Gammon, Betsy 48-51
Gardeners 149
Gardening 77-80
Germany 134, 145
Gittisham 56
Glasgow, Countess 93
Gloucester 84
Goodenough, Revd 81
Grant, Mrs 44
Greenway 139
Griffiths, Amelia 80-2; Amelia Elizabeth 82; William 81

Hamilton, Anne 38-40
Hannington, Miss 40
Harvey, William Henry 80

Hayne, Joseph 43
Henett, John 93
Hercules 17-18
Hill, Roger 32
Hodges, Maude 143
Hole, John 26
Holland 45; people of 45
Holman, Elizabeth 1, 67-72; Simon 70
Holne 52
Holsworthy 143
Honiton 44, 48, 143, 144
Hooker, John 3
Hopping, Edward 66
Horses 79
Hoskins, W. G. 24
Howey, Elsie 113-115, 115-117
Hubbard, Old Mother 59-65
Hunt, Miss 45
Hurd, Sarah 24

Iceland 13
Ilfracombe 49-52, 55, 143; museum 51
India, Bombay 70
Ireland 13, 44
Ironside, Eva 145
Italy 55, San Vitale 55

Jamaica 87
Jews 56, 87
Joan of Arc 115
Johnson, Cornelius 11

Kenney, Jessie 113-115
Kent 9
Kingsford-Lethbridge, Amy 143
Kingsley, Charles 80-1, 140
Kitley 59

Langhorne, family 132
Languages 44
Lazenby, Katherine 143
Leach, Bernard 137
Lewis, Mr 83; Wyndham 84-5
Lloyd, Temperance 6
Lock, Peter 25
London 11, 12, 20, 43, 53, 54, 99, 115, 119, 122, 123-4, 149; Covent Garden 43; Drury Lane 43; Fortnum &

Mason 86; Globe Theatre 137; Hyde Park 117, 119; Queen's Theatre 137; shop girls 98; West End 138
Lynton 113; Hollerday House 113

Maclennan, Jean 145
Maconochie, Margaret 142
Macready, William 43
Malaprop, Mrs 72
Malta 124
Martel, Nellie 111-112
Martin, Sarah Catherine 59-65
McMillan, Annie 119
McTaggart, Anne 38, 40
Medicine 123-6, 127-30, 143-5
Memorial 21-2
Methodism 57-8
Militia 51
Mill, John Stuart 125
Mincemeat 6
Mohamet Basha 48
Mol, Thomas 24
Mol's Coffee House 2, 23-4
Moore, Henry 137
More, Hannah 53
Moreman, Annis 29; Christopher 31; Mrs 38; Thomasin 25-37; Wilmot 25-37
Moretonhampstead 143
Mosley, Oswald 134
Murch, Mary 24

National College of Domestic Subjects 98
Navvies 67-72
Navy 66, 101-7
Neve, Annie 90-1
Newton Abbot 16, 20-22, 109, 110-112, 143
Nicholson, Ben 137; Winifred 137
North Molton 25
Northampton, Apethorpe 9, 12
Northcote, Stafford 85
Nymet Tracey 26

Okehampton 143
Orchard, Lieut. Col. 51
Otterton 79

Ottery St Mary 56, 81, 143, 144
Oyster women 13

Paignton 90-1, 149
Pankhurst, Emmeline 108, 110-112,
   120-3, 136, 144; Sylvia 122
Parkhouse, Hannah 53; Philip 53
Parliament 73-6
Parminter, Elizabeth 55; Jane 55-6;
   Mary 55-6
Parr, Olive Katherine 140-2; Mrs 141
Partington, Mrs 72-6
Paton, Private C. H. 130
Pearce, Thomas 67
Peek, Augusta 143
Perriam, Anne 2, 65-7
Pharmaceutical Society 90
Phillips, Juanita 143, 144; Phillips,
   Mary 115-117; Thomas 144
Pickard, Jonathan 12
Pilgrimage 110, 117-119
Pilton 81
Plymouth 20, 40-1, 99, 102-7, 108, 109,
   118-119, 120-1, 122-3, 126, 132-4,
   143, 148; Chief Constable 120, 134-5;
   Corn Exchange 119; Dispensary
   124-5; Great Western Docks, 121;
   Hoe 109; magistrates 70; North Hill
   118; police 70; Smeaton's Tower 109;
   Soroptomists 126; Stoke Dameral
   104; Torpoint ferry 118; Victoria
   Park 119; Weston Mill 105
Point in View 55-6
Polwhele, Richard 44
Portland, Duke of 51
Prince, John 3
Printers 27
Pynes 85

Railways 67-71
Raleigh, Sir Walter 23-4
Ramsay, Mabel 108-9, 118-119, 123-6,
   134; Mrs 119, 126
Recipe books 6
Reigate 91
Reynell, Lucy 20-22; Richard 20-22
Reynolds, Alice 26
Rice, Mr 131-2

Roberts, Margaret 93
Robertson, Miss 125
Rogers, family 81
Rolfe, Gwendolyn 145
Rolle, John 78; Louisa 77-80
Roosevelt, Eleanor 137; Franklin 137
Rose, Philip 87
Rowing 19
Russia 150; Royal Family 86

Sandwich, Countess 93
Scotland 44, 124; Edinburgh 44, 145;
   Inverness 44
Scott, Granny 49-52
Seaton 142
Seaweed 80-2
Sebag-Montefiorie, Ida 142
Sewing 22
Sex 132
Shaldon 13-19
Sheridan, Richard 53
Sheriff, R. C. 136
Shillaber, Benjamin Penhallow 72
Shiloh 58
Ships, S. S. Majestic 120, 136
Siddons, Sarah 53
Sidmouth 72-6, 119; Chit Rock 76
Sidwella, St 4
Simcoe, Caroline 48; Charlotte
   47; Eliza 45; Elizabeth 45-8, 49;
   Governor 45-8; Harriet 47
Skinner, Caroline 2, 91-8, 107; Emily 2,
   91-8, 107; John 13-14, 18. 19
Skirrow, Florence 143
Slapton 51
Slavery 76, 108
Smith, George Charles 102; Sydney 73
Somerset, Taunton 73-4, 119
Soroptomists 126
Southcott, Joanna 56-8
Southleigh 26
Spencer, Countess 93
Stalin, Josef 133
Stammwitz, Louisa 90-1
Stanhope, Charles 43
Stanley, Maude 94
Stockton-on-Tees 91
Stokeinteignhead 13

Storms 73-6
Strikes 131-2
Suffrage movement 107-26, 134, 143, 144
Sunderland 71
Surrey, Hindhead 104-5
Sutherland, Duchess 93
Suttie, Lieut. 52
Swete, John 18, 44
Symes, Deborah 6
Symons, Miss 119

Taleford 56
Tawstock, 9-12
Taxi drivers 146, 148-9
Teignmouth 1, 13-19
Temperance 100-104, 132-4
Terry, Ellen 54
Thursby, Vice Admiral 105
Tiverton 38, 52, 53-4, 143
Toplady, Augustus 16
Topsham 119
Torbay, Babbacombe 2, 91-8, 143; Braddon Hill 86-9; Babbacombe 2, 91-8, 143; Ferny Combe 92-8; Ferny Bank 92-8; Ferny Hollow 95-6; Florence Villa 98; Meadfoot Road 82; Natural History Society 82; Royal Hotel 86; Sutherland Tower 93; Torquay 7, 13, 80-2, 86-9, 90-1, 115, 119, 138, 143; Torwood 82; Warberry Hill 93
Totnes 137
Trefusis, Eva 143; family 78
Trembles, Mary 6
Turkey 48; Constantinople 48
Turner, J. M. W. 76

Ugbrooke 89
United States 44, 120, 126, 132, 135, 137, 138; navy 105; New England 13, 72; New York 135, 136; Washington D.C. 135

Upholstery shop 56-7

van Dyck, Anthony 11
Vean, Private 128
Verneer, Ida 98
Vicary, Eleanor 143
Victoria, Queen 78, 86, 88
Vikings 52
Vinnicombe, Mrs 24
Virgil 77
Voluntary Aid Detachment 127-30, 138, 145

Wales 49; Cardiff 71, 85; Newport 70-1
War, American Civil 132; Civil 11-12, 21; first world 109, 123, 125, 127-30, 135, 141, 143-5, 151-2; second world 98, 134-5, 145-50
Watermouth Castle 143
Watters, Private H. 128
Wellington, Duke of 76
Wentworth, Vera 113-115, 115-117
Wesley, Mary 3
Weston, Agatha 2, 99-107, 133
Westward Ho! 113
Whitaker, Evelyn 95-6
White Knights 141
Whitney family 135
Widecombe-In-The-Moor 140-2
Wildier, Margaret 24
Wildy, Mary 24
Wilkes, John 39
Willoughby, Lord 88
Willyams, Sarah Brydges 86-9, 90
Wintz, Sophia 2, 99-107
Witchcraft 6
Wollstonecraft, Mary 39
Women, history of 1-7; population in Devon 5; teachers 7
Wyatt, Mary 82